First
Edition

Online Enrollment Management

Using For-Profit Best Practices at Non-Profit Colleges

James L. Dunn, M.A.Ed.
The Learning House, Inc.

ISBN 978-0-557-56141-4

DESIGNER

Krystle Feathers

EDITORS

Audrey Kessler
Stanimira Stefanova

PROOFREADER

Hannah Hanson

PUBLISHER

The Learning House, Inc.

ABOUT THE AUTHOR

James L. Dunn, M.A.Ed.

Mr. Dunn has worked in the field of enrollment management for nearly 15 years, specializing in online and adult education. He has served as a highly successful and award-winning director of enrollment and admissions for some of the largest and most successful for-profit higher education institutions in the United States, including the University of Phoenix and Kaplan Higher Education Corporation.

Mr. Dunn has also served as the president of American Education Consultants, LLC, which specializes in online and adult education enrollment management consulting.

Born in Cincinnati, Ohio, in 1968, Mr. Dunn attended Northern Kentucky University and Excelsior College as an undergraduate and has a Bachelor of Science in Liberal Studies with dual concentrations in history and political science. He has also earned a Master of Arts in Education from the University of Phoenix.

CONTENTS

FOREWORD

Admissions have turned into sales...

At The Learning House, Inc., we have worked with small private schools over the past 10 years to help them start, manage, and expand their online programs. During that time, we have seen several schools develop their programs and replace declining institutional giving with tuition revenue from online programs while fulfilling their mission and increasing their program offerings to qualified and gifted students who could not attend traditionally. However, even as these schools have broadened their ability to serve their communities by offering online degree programs and courses, they have fallen behind for-profit institutions. Traditional schools, including our partners, have repeatedly failed to recognize what for-profit institutions consider fundamental: Admissions are "sales."

Upon receiving an inquiry from a potential student, for-profit schools will respond within 15 minutes. They will call the "leads" and stay on the phone with them until the leads understand what they must do to obtain their chosen degree. The for-profit school will help them assemble their application packets and assist them through the maze of financial aid. The school will provisionally admit these students into their college and sign them up for their first class. For-profit enrollment counselors do all of this on the first call, if possible. Within less than 1 hour, the leads will be signed up for their first class and likely start the college's program within 30 days. Compare this to the standard admissions process at a typical traditional school and you will see some scary results! We have worked with more than 100 traditional schools and none of them—even the best—can serve the potential student as well.

Learning House was founded on the principle of helping traditional schools evolve and stay competitive as the world around them rapidly changes. With this purpose in mind, we sought out and recruited James Dunn to help us, and we commissioned him to write this book. Jim is a lifelong enrollment manager who brings remarkable for-profit admissions expertise from well-known and successful for-profit schools such as Kaplan and the University of Phoenix. In the following pages, Jim shares many of the secrets of these large for-profit behemoths. We hope that the tips and strategies Jim unfolds in this book will aid you in reshaping your admissions programs while at the same time preserving what makes your school unique and special.

Good luck!

Steven A. Huey
Chief Operating Officer
The Learning House, Inc.

Introduction

In the spring of 2008, someone asked me an interesting question: Why do you think the large for-profit colleges, such as the University of Phoenix and Kaplan University, have had so much success while so many of the well-respected, private non-profit colleges have struggled in the online market? The question piqued my interest, and I thought I knew the answer.

As an example of just how successful the large for-profit institutions have become, the University of Phoenix is expected to surpass 440,000 students and has grown into one of the largest and most profitable higher-education institutions in the world. The 2009 revenue reported by the Apollo Group (the parent company of the University of Phoenix) surpassed $3.9 billion (Apollo Group, 2009). With 440,000 students, the University of Phoenix has captured almost 9.7% of the 4.6 million online students in the United States (Allen & Seaman, 2010).

After working as a director of enrollment for both the University of Phoenix and Kaplan Higher Education Corporation and knowing how much time, energy, and money they devote to recruiting efforts, my first instinct was to give the obvious answer: marketing. Institutions such as these spend millions of dollars each year to ensure that their name pervades the Internet, even to the point where one might have difficulty finding a Web site without an online college banner advertisement.

The marketing answer, however, was too obvious. I had worked for several for-profit colleges over the years and began to realize that I only saw one side of the industry. By the spring of 2009, I was ready to leave the University of Phoenix in search of another challenge. The world of non-profit online education began to intrigue me, and I recognized the untapped recruiting potential hidden within the media markets of non-profit institutions.

untapped   recruiting   potential

I wanted a new challenge, but I could not escape two fundamental questions: What were these non-profit institutions doing wrong? Why were they falling so far behind? The answer had to involve more than a simple lack of marketing. The questions roused my curiosity and compelled me to find the answer. In 2009, I launched my own enrollment consulting company and decided to help these non-profit colleges and universities reach their online enrollment goals.

> **What were these non-profit institutions doing wrong? Why were they falling so far behind?**

Unfortunately, when I saw firsthand how the non-profit colleges had structured their online enrollment divisions, I was shocked at what I found. The for-profit institutions were not winning the battle for online students because they dominated the Internet or because they poured massive amounts of cash into national marketing campaigns. They were winning because the non-profit institutions refused to accept that the world had changed. The non-profit institutions failed to notice that enrollment management had evolved into a sophisticated science and an intricate art. To survive and thrive in the online arena, the non-profit institutions had to take heed.

More often than not, I found that the non-profit institutions either refused to recognize how college recruiting had changed during the information revolution or refused to adopt the new standards and practices needed to build a successful online program. They needed a complete overhaul of staffing, organizational structure, management, marketing, enrollment strategy, and retention.

A complete overhaul was necessary:

☑ staffing

☑ organizational structure

☑ management

☑ marketing

☑ enrollment strategy

☑ retention

By the summer of 2009, I began working with a company called The Learning House, Inc. The company was formed in 2001 by Dr. Denzil Edge with the primary mission of helping small independent colleges and universities develop, market, and launch their own online degree programs. Learning House had formed partnerships with more than 70 independent, non-profit colleges across the country. The company soon learned that many of these schools would need a dramatic shift in vision and structure to turn their basic online classes into profitable, self-sustaining, online degree programs. The more I learned about the company, the more I realized that Learning House could help the non-profit market develop programs that would surpass the for-profit colleges in quality and allow independent colleges to compete with the for-profit colleges in their local markets.

LEARNINGHOUSE™
Your Online Education Partner

All the resources and knowledge to design and customize every aspect of an **effective** online education program.

I had found in one place all of the pieces needed for success—namely, a partner that could provide technical expertise, an affordable learning management system, curriculum assistance, and marketing savvy. The next step would involve a bigger challenge: convincing the non-profit institutions that the world had changed. They had to realize that students, marketing strategies, recruiting best practices, and staffing models had all changed in the last few years.

We had a difficult task ahead of us. It began with a review of several independent non-profit institutions that had contracted with Learning House. We planned to study staffing models, conversions, online department structure, and marketing plans and build a new model based on for-profit best practices. On paper, the plan sounded simple. It soon became clear that the task would prove much more difficult than anticipated because the variables for evaluation did not exist.

Many of the non-profit colleges had no separate online enrollment staff, no online enrollment plan, and no online support staff. At best, some of the schools had one person in charge of the school's online enrollment program, but that person usually lacked expertise in the field. Credentials ranged from the director of academic affairs or an online faculty member to a part-time student employee or a retired English literature professor working 10 hours a week for the school's admissions department. Several colleges fared slightly better, having placed their online enrollment goals under the umbrella of their traditional admissions department. Far more typically, however, many colleges employed untrained traditional enrollment counselors. While perhaps fully prepared to handle their face-to-face enrollment campaigns and marketing efforts, these colleges did not have the resources to handle online enrollment.

> Online enrollment management and traditional enrollment management require different approaches for everything from staffing levels and staff qualifications to management and staff duties.

Online enrollment management and traditional enrollment management require different approaches for everything from staffing levels and staff qualifications to management and staff duties. This book is designed to not only help identify those differences and guide college administrators as they seriously reconsider their online program planning efforts but also to encourage them to become online enrollment champions at their institutions.

The goal is to help non-profit educational institutions dominate their local market for online learning opportunities. They do not have to try to compete with the large for-profit institutions on a national level. I just want to help them at least own their own backyard.

> The goal is to help non-profit educational institutions dominate their local market.

Chapter One

The Fundamentals

This chapter covers the following **key points**:

» Importance of online programs

» Revenue from online programs

» The six components of an online program plan:

- Program selection
- Program term
- Learning management system selection
- Cost of instruction
- Support staff
- Advertising and student acquisition costs

When evaluating an online operating and enrollment model, we begin by asking the educational institution's president the following questions: Why do you want your college to offer online programs? Is it because you want additional revenue to construct new buildings and purchase new equipment for your college? Is it because you want to give your brick-and-mortar students a more flexible scheduling option and increase retention and graduation rates? After receiving their answer, we would then ask this pointed question: Do you want to have an online *presence*, or do you want to become an online *player*?

If you want the former, then this book is not for you. Simply having a presence in the online educational arena will not likely create a significant revenue source. In our experience, you need carefully selected, well-planned, appropriately staffed, and fully online degree programs to generate substantial revenue over a long period.

> You need carefully selected, well-planned, appropriately staffed, and fully online degree programs to generate substantial revenue.

The following story illustrates the dichotomy of the two approaches to online learning: A college dean of enrollment told me that he did not want to offer online programs—just single courses. He said, "Everyone knows that if a college offers a program completely online, they are just doing it for the money." I looked at him for a few seconds and struggled to find a suitable reply. My answer was simple and to the point: "Yes, salaries cost money; buildings cost money; electricity, water, and heat all cost money." He smiled at me and replied, "We always find a way to pay the bills, and we do not have to sell our souls to do it." He turned around with his head held high and walked away. I was stunned. His thinking, while perhaps well intentioned, was quite naive.

**revenue
is not
evil**

This story leads me to my next point: Revenue is not evil. For years, educational professionals have tossed around the terms *non-profit* and *for-profit* as if using them to separate the innocent, pure, and well-intentioned "real colleges" of the world from the evil, money-hungry diploma mills. The non-profit designation primarily refers to an organization's Internal Revenue Service tax-liability—nothing more. All private, independent colleges and universities operate under the same principle: Revenue is necessary to keep the doors open, pay salaries, construct new buildings, and buy new equipment.

Based on the assumption that revenue is not evil, this chapter focuses on six basic components of an online program plan designed to generate maximum revenue with reasonable expenses and without sacrificing the quality of instruction. The six focus areas are program selection, program term, learning management system selection, cost of instruction, support staff, and advertising and student acquisition costs. Schools must also consider numerous other issues—such as accreditation, curriculum development, and learning outcomes—but this chapter focuses on the issues most directly related to operations and enrollment management.

1 Program Selection

**Which programs do you
want to offer online,
and why?**

For this chapter, I will assume that you want to become an online player with the ability to reap the rewards that accompany the role. The next question is this: "Which programs do you want to offer online, and why? " When I first asked college administrators this question, I received some surprising answers. One administrator said he wanted to make a particular program available online because "the faculty really liked it." Another administrator said his program selections "fit the image of the school." Nobody specified, however, how these programs catered to the wants and needs of students living within a 50-mile radius of the institution. I explained to one administrator that most online students enroll in an online college—even a large for-profit institution—that has a brick-and-mortar location within 50 miles of their homes (Allen & Seaman, 2008). Schools must not take lightly the selection of their online programs. More is at stake than simply making the college part of the national scene or catering to the whims of faculty. Schools should select programs that will attract a large share of the online student population within their 50-mile marketing radius. One reason the University of Phoenix grew so quickly is because it opened branch campuses and learning centers across the country. The school's leaders understood that nothing served as a substitute for having a local presence; the success of their ground-campus network gives credence to their strategy.

> Schools must not take lightly the selection of their online programs. More is at stake than simply making the college part of the national scene or catering to the whims of faculty.

Selecting the right program for the local market is actually quite simple—and it does not involve hiring a marketing company to research the school's 50-mile coverage area. It also does not require the school to survey the population or rely on anecdotal evidence about program interests. Administrators need to look no further than their school's database. School administrators need to determine which primary programs have generated the most requests for information from individuals who live within 50 miles of the college. The strategy works because most online students start at a ground campus within the school's 50-mile radius.

Most private colleges have spent years building a positive reputation in their communities and often receive a large number of requests for information about their brick-

and-mortar programs. Most colleges have hundreds, if not thousands, of non-converted requests for information in their school's database. These brick-and-mortar leads represent the online students of tomorrow. To mine this trove of information, you must ask two basic questions about these individuals: Which programs have sparked the most interest? Which programs did these prospective students ultimately select?

Make sure you gather and analyze information requests only from prospective students who live within the school's 50-mile radius. Many colleges have niche programs for online program growth that attract requests for information from people across the country; however, these may not be your school's best-producing, local online programs. If your niche programs don't draw a significant number of leads from the school's 50-mile radius, focus on the programs that do.

> If your niche programs don't draw a significant number of leads from the school's 50-mile radius, focus on the programs that do.

2 Program Term

Let us assume that you have completed your research and found that your bachelor's degree program in management has generated a significant amount of interest within your market. Now you want to offer it online. From an enrollment and marketing perspective, prospective students must see the term length as highly desirable. Your research also likely showed that most online candidates are working adults. As a result, you will find that the primary reason students choose online learning is for convenience. Therefore, you should always use the convenience aspect of online learning as part of your marketing arsenal to enhance its effectiveness. Many institutions fail to follow this advice and do so at their peril.

For example, a college administrator told me that her school had designed its online program "only in the best interest of the student." She insisted that students should enroll in a 16-week term and register for multiple courses to have full-time status and receive a true "college experience."

This thinking, however, is flawed. The U.S. Department of Education states that students must be enrolled for a minimum of 24 credit hours and 30 weeks of instruction to be considered full-time (Burkhardt & Deeken, n.d.). Institutions of higher education use dozens of term options, including 16-week semesters, 4-week modular terms, 8-week blocks, and 9-week quarters. All of these terms can support full-time status and serve a specific student demographic.

Using the University of Phoenix as an example, the school offers a 9-week, two-course block for its associate programs; a 5-week, one-course block for its undergraduate (bachelor's) programs; and a 6-week, one-course block for its master-level courses. The school has a simple rationale for these term lengths: More than 400,000 students view the terms as convenient. The University of Phoenix discovered that students wanted these term lengths in every state, in every market, and for every program.

Learning Management System Selection 3

This book does not cover in detail the options for learning management systems and/or site-hosting providers, because it primarily focuses on the enrollment management aspect of online education. After all, students do not choose a college based on its learning management platform. The platform itself matters only secondarily.

> Students do not choose a college based on its learning management platform.

> **The start-up costs, around-the-clock technical support, Web site maintenance, and staff training matter more than the platform.**

From the institution's perspective, the start-up costs, around-the-clock technical support, Web site maintenance, and staff training matter more than the platform. Nothing will drain a school's operating budget more than an online learning system that only meets faculty specifications. Instead, the school should focus on the system's efficiency, affordability, and ease of use. Too often, colleges spend years digging themselves out of debt as a result of poor planning, poor research, and inadequate fiscal discipline. A large state college may use a particular learning management system, but that does not necessarily make it the right choice for your school. You would do much better to select an affordable system with low start-up costs and invest more money in student acquisition, marketing, enrollment counselors, and support staff.

These insights came to me when I began working as the director of online operations for a small non-profit college (which had little or no money to invest) after spending most of my career with for-profit colleges. I knew I would need to find a company to help me develop and host the school's online program as well as set up and maintain the selected learning management system. My school would also need help with online marketing. After considerable research, I chose Learning House for several reasons. First, I sought a company that would provide all of the services I needed with as little start-up costs as possible. Second, I sought qualified curriculum developers because the school's faculty needed help converting ground programs into an online format. Third, I knew the staff would require training on how to use the learning management system and provide and maintain around-the-clock technical support. Fourth, I knew I would need assistance in developing a dedicated online college Web site and Internet marketing plan.

Learning House submitted a proposal that charged no up-front fees but provided all of the elements required for a successful online learning environment. Companies such as Learning House charge the school a per-enrollment fee only after students have enrolled in and started the class.

The learning management system I sought needed to accomplish the following:

- Provide a secure environment through unique user names and passwords
- Deliver content and multimedia
- Provide attendance data and reports on each student enrolled in each course
- Provide the registrar, administrators, and instructors with access to the back end of the learning management system
- Enable students to direct questions to an instructor through embedded e-mail
- Enable faculty to send e-mail to an individual student or to all students
- Enable faculty and students to post questions on a discussion board
- Enable faculty and students to talk with each other in chat rooms
- Enable students to take quizzes, pre-tests, and post-test exams
- Enable faculty to post announcements and a calendar for each course
- Enable faculty to offer Internet links, frequently asked questions, and other references
- Enable faculty to organize students into teams
- Enable faculty to organize student work through the teams function
- Provide a unique portal reflecting the look and feel of the online campus
- Maintain a grade book of exams for each instructor
- Enable faculty to update and change content within a course
- Enable faculty to use presentation software
- Enable faculty to conduct surveys of student opinions
- Enable faculty to grade essay exams within the learning management system
- Enable faculty to deliver instruction through a live virtual classroom

Always look for value in a learning management system. Do your research, and consider your options. Remember, students do not choose a college based on its learning management system. The value lies not in what your system can do for you but in what you can do with the system that will help your institution succeed.

Cost of Instruction

The COI or cost of instruction is an important factor in any online program. You might consider hiring adjunct instructors rather than full-time faculty members to teach most of your online courses; doing so can keep costs low. Some administrators insist that their programs are so special that they would prefer to have only full-time faculty members teach the online courses. Such thinking misses the point. Highly qualified instructors capable of teaching online courses are available throughout the country. They have just as many credentials as those of an institution's full-time faculty and will cost you much less.

> (Adjuncts) have just as many credentials as those of an institution's full-time faculty and will cost you much less.

For example, I once took a graduate-level military history class online. My instructor was a West Point graduate with a master's degree in U.S. history from Columbia University and a doctorate from Georgetown University. He had worked for the Department of Defense for 25 years, and he had recently retired and wanted to teach from home. Surely he was qualified to teach an introductory online history course. Unfortunately, many non-profit colleges turned him down because he was not a member of their full-time faculty.

Although highly qualified adjunct instructors command a lower salary, they can bring prestige to an institution. From an operational, educational, and fiscal perspective, adjunct instructors serve as the perfect solution for an online college that wants to maximize its earnings and lower its cost of instruction. Using adjunct instructors lets everyone win.

Support Staff 5

College staffing can be a frustrating task as various departments vie for additional staff, pitting one department against the other and often pulling the chief financial officer or budget manager in different directions. For-profit educational institutions tend to focus more on the front end, ensuring that they always have fully staffed enrollment departments; non-profit institutions, however, tend to focus more on the back end, ensuring that they have adequate academic support. Both types of institutions, however, share a lack of qualified financial counselors. To succeed on all levels, colleges need to invest in all three positions—enrollment counselors, academic support, and financial counselors—but they rarely do so.

> To succeed on all levels, colleges need to invest in all three positions—enrollment counselors, academic support, and financial counselors.

 Enrollment Staffing

The enrollment counselor position is critical to the online program's success. When I worked at the University of Phoenix, campus directors hired nearly 100 enrollment counselors for just one campus location. Colleges such as Phoenix understand that a request for information from a student does not lead to an enrollment on its own; they know that they must assign trained, competent staff to work on the front end of the process. For every 100 new students per year, a typical for-profit educational institution will have at least one enrollment counselor to service them. Many of the non-profit colleges I have

> A typical for-profit enrollment counselor can efficiently handle a caseload of only 100 new students a year.

worked with considered themselves lucky to have even one counselor for every 200 new online enrollments. A typical for-profit enrollment counselor can efficiently handle a caseload of only 100 new students a year, given the duties of his or her job. An industry standard, however, does not exist for the level of staffing needed to achieve success in an online learning environment.

Depending on an institution's application process and support teams, enrollment counselors' productivity can vary. Therefore, you absolutely must know your average enrollment and manage your staffing levels accordingly. If your enrollment counselors produce significantly more than 100 enrollments per year, you might need to increase staffing; not doing so could mean losing students who otherwise might have enrolled. For a situation where greater individual production leads to the loss of institutional enrollments, consider the following example: Assume that you have only one enrollment counselor and that person has a yearly average of 100 new enrollments. Now assume that this same counselor enrolls 150 students this year. That increase is significant, but it doesn't tell the whole story.

A counselor working with that many students probably does not have enough hours in the day to contact every lead in the system. By hiring an additional counselor, you might be able to produce 200 new enrollments per year by more efficiently working all the leads in your database. The revenue generated from the additional 50 students can more than compensate for the increase in expenditure for the new employee's salary.

It is a delicate balance. Schools base their enrollment staffing levels on an expected average number of new enrollments per counselor per year. This represents a typical for-profit model, and it works incredibly well.

 Academic Support Staffing

For-profit educational institutions tend to not do as well in the area of servicing students after classes begin. Some of the larger online colleges have an incredibly high ratio of students to academic counselors. This high student-to-academic counselor ratio is one of the primary reasons why for-profits have such a bad reputation. Imagine a school the size of the University of Phoenix with more than 440,000 students. Now imagine how many counselors it would take to support that population. Based on a standard ratio of 100:1, the school would need 4,400 academic counselors. The lack of back-end academic support represents the one area where non-profit colleges have the advantage over the larger for-profit institutions. Good service always has value, and the colleges that understand this and staff accordingly will have an ideal selling point when enrollment counselors talk to potential students.

 Financial Staffing

Unfortunately, both for-profit institutions and non-profit institutions are equally shortsighted when it comes to staffing financial counselors. In today's world of higher loan default rates and a struggling economy, colleges of all sizes need to pay close attention to the happenings in our nation's capital and with the Department of Education. The days of private lending to students have ended, and the age of direct lending from the Department of Education has begun.

Most colleges rely heavily on disbursements from Title IV Stafford Loan and Pell Grant programs.

Educational institutions could not function without Title
IV eligibility, and they need to place more importance
on staffing levels in this area. Maintaining a student-
to-financial counselor ratio of at least 200:1 no longer
constitutes a luxury; it is quickly becoming a necessity for
successful institutions. Maintaining this ratio will increase
student-satisfaction ratings and retention rates while
ensuring the institution's continued operation.

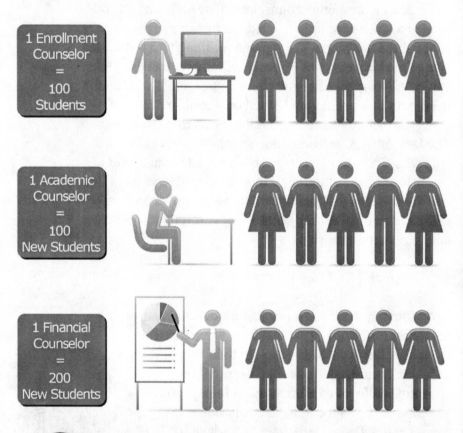

1 Enrollment
Counselor
=
100
Students

1 Academic
Counselor
=
100
New Students

1 Financial
Counselor
=
200
New Students

6 Advertising and Student Acquisition Costs

One of the most confusing and misunderstood aspects
of developing a revenue plan is the task of estimating
advertising and student acquisition costs. Many college

administrators fail to understand that unless they know how many enrollments come from each type, source, and category of marketing—including the cost per lead, application, and completed enrollment—they cannot determine an advertising cost per enrollment figure. Finding these numbers requires time and effort, but the task matters greatly.

The objective is to spend money only where the expenditure of funds has produced results. Remember that every college—even a non-profit institution—is a business, and those in charge must manage it according to sound business practices. We will cover this topic in greater detail in a later chapter.

Chapter Summary

This chapter distinguished between having an online presence and being an online player. In doing so, it emphasized the importance of developing carefully selected, well-planned, and appropriately staffed online degree programs designed to generate substantial revenue over a long period. This chapter also discussed the six basic components of an online program: program selection, program term, learning management system selection, cost of instruction, support staff, and advertising and student acquisition costs.

Chapter Two

The Enrollment Counselor

This chapter covers the following **key points**:

» Responsibilities of enrollment counselors
» Steps for hiring enrollment counselors
» Guide for training online enrollment counselors

When I visited a college recently to help the administration determine why the school's enrollment for online programs was not growing, an administrator insisted the staff had done "all the right things." They had decided to become a player in the online market and had prepared themselves to invest the money needed to start the program. They had selected two high-demand programs in their immediate market and planned to offer classes in 6-week blocks for the convenience of working adults. They were also investing in marketing campaigns that brought in a high volume of leads. They had a good strategy, but students were not enrolling.

> An administrator insisted the staff had done "all the right things."

After further inquiry, I found that the college lacked any effective initial-contact strategy for working with its leads. Its only strategy involved sending an automatically generated e-mail thanking students for their interest and directing them to the school's Web site for more information on how to complete the online application.

If I had heard this a year ago, I would have been shocked. I would have considered it an anomaly. However, now I realize that while this strategy is doomed to fail, many non-profit colleges follow it. So many non-profit educational institutions do not understand that the enrollment process runs on a specific cycle that begins when a student requests information. Administrators at many small non-profit educational institutions stop listening to me when we reach this point in the conversation. They bemoan the lack of staff to call every lead and the budget constraints that preclude the hiring of additional personnel to handle the volume. It is a vicious cycle, and they have no clue how to solve the problem.

> The enrollment process runs on a specific cycle that begins when a student requests information.

Imagine trying to run a restaurant without cooks. You invest thousands of dollars in a state-of-the-art kitchen, stock it with the best ingredients, hire service staff, and spend even more money on décor and fine china, but no food comes out of the kitchen. The answer to the puzzle is simple: Without people to prepare the ingredients, you will never have food to serve. No matter how many ingredients you bring into the kitchen, a main dish will not magically appear; you cannot blame the ingredients.

> **Leads are not the same as enrollments. Leads are the raw material of enrollments.**

Blaming the ingredients occurs at virtually dozens of small non-profit colleges. Administrators honestly believe that students will appear magically from the marketing dollars they expend. If a school could do this so easily, then the University of Phoenix would have more than 10 million students. Unfortunately, leads are not the same as enrollments. Leads are the raw material of enrollments. You must nurture, respect, and invest a considerable amount of time in each lead before it can become an enrollment.

So, who has the responsibility of sorting through the leads, finding the prospects who are truly interested in enrolling, helping them through the enrollment process, and turning these leads into enrollments? A highly trained, dedicated, and professional enrollment staff performs this job. The basic principle of enrollment success is staffing, staffing, staffing. It serves as the foundation of effective online enrollment management. No online educational institution will ever reach its potential without understanding this principle.

> **The basic principle of enrollment success is staffing, staffing, staffing.**

Enrollment Counselor Basics

The titles run the gamut from admissions representative to admissions counselor to enrollment counselor. The title, however, means nothing in an online enrollment environment. An online enrollment counselor has little in common with a traditional brick-and-mortar counselor. The two differ in many ways: job description, daily expectations, training methods, and qualifications. Many school administrators erroneously believe that because they have a successful traditional enrollment team, their online team will succeed as well. Nothing is further from the truth. Indeed, many of the qualities that prove helpful for traditional enrollment counselors prove detrimental in an online enrollment setting.

Everything is different: leads, students' expectations, marketing approaches, data-capture procedures, contact strategy, interview process, follow-up procedures, and—perhaps most importantly— the day-to-day activities and expectations of an online enrollment team. If your online counselors are not prepared to spend at least 5 hours a day on the telephone, they will never reach their potential and service all of the leads you have generated. Online enrollment is more about contacting and bonding with individual students than it is about selling the school, which means that time spent with each student is incredibly important.

> Online enrollment is more about contacting and bonding with individual students than it is about selling the school, which means that time spent with each student is incredibly important.

Given the nature of online education, the process always has a sense of remoteness that you cannot overcome completely. However, you can make great strides if you remember this: Those who bond will win. Most students shop several schools with online programs before making a decision and, unlike the traditional process that might involve weeks of campus visits and interviews, the online world moves at lightning speed. Decisions are made in hours and days, not weeks and months. Students can, and will, request information from several schools in a matter of minutes. They seek someone to help them make a decision, and they want help with the process. More than that, they want guidance from someone who does not just take orders.

The first college to contact the student, answer the student's questions, show the student what to do next, and become the student's champion usually reaps an enrollment. Many non-profit educational institutions may not want to hear this, but students do not consider a college's tradition and great reputation as primary factors when choosing an online college. Likewise, tuition and reputation do not serve as the primary selling points for online enrollment staff. Speed and urgency mean much more to the online student. If you do not contact your leads, a for-profit institution surely will. Remember, those who bond will win.

Those who bond will win.

For many colleges, this constitutes a completely new way of thinking, which many consider unsettling. Simply put, for-profit institutions are hunting. Consider this: The University of Phoenix is projected to have more than 440,000 students enrolled in 2010. Are their programs better than yours? Are they more respected? Are their instructors better than yours? Are they less expensive? If you have pride in your programs and in your college, you should answer most of these questions with a resounding "no." Why have their programs dominated every market?

How do they keep growing every year at a phenomenal rate? They do not grow faster because they have better marketing. The University of Phoenix and all of the other for-profit institutions stand out because they have focused their resources on enrollment counselor staffing levels while embracing a fundamental rule of online recruiting: Those who bond will win.

The University of Phoenix does not operate according to a new enrollment strategy. They did not invent the concept; they simply mastered it. I started working in the for-profit education industry in 1996 and have seen the same rule applied on every campus, in every state, and for every program. For-profit colleges take the time to hire and train their staff to understand this principle. Their willingness to do so acts as the driving force behind their success. The enrollment counselor serves as the first point of contact and the engine behind enrollment growth. Do not forget or dismiss the position of enrollment counselor as inconsequential. Without enrollment counselors, you have no cooks in your kitchen.

> The enrollment counselor serves as the first point of contact and the engine behind enrollment growth.

Hiring the Enrollment Counselor

One of the biggest mistakes I have seen at both for-profit and non-profit educational institutions pertains to hiring. If you do not hire well, your costs skyrocket, your revenue drops, your morale deteriorates, and your students suffer. Many for-profit enrollment departments (including the University of Phoenix) face the significant issue of staff turnover. Enrollment counselors at for-profit institutions work in a high-pressure environment all day, every day. However, people do not leave their jobs because of this pressure. They leave because the pressure is not what they expected.

Online Enrollment Management

The two basic rules of hiring a successful online enrollment counselor are to look for the proper personality traits and set the proper expectations.

Without exception, every successful campus has one unmistakable component: The managers hire well. The two basic rules of hiring a successful online enrollment counselor are to look for the proper personality traits and set the proper expectations. It may sound easy, but it is the hardest assignment many managers will undertake during their careers.

All managers who have plowed through a pile of resumes will have developed their own techniques over the years to speed up the selection process. Since I have spent the majority of my adult life in enrollment management, I have a cut-and-dried system. I look for something much more important than educational background, degree level, time in previous jobs, or enrollment experience. I focus on the amount of time the applicant spent on the telephone at previous jobs, because enrollment counselors will spend more than 50% of their day making telephone calls.

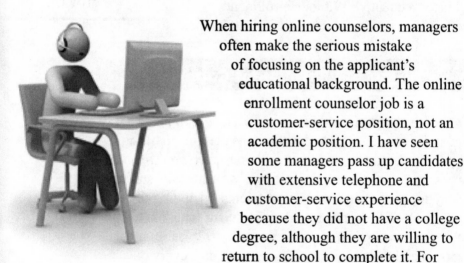

When hiring online counselors, managers often make the serious mistake of focusing on the applicant's educational background. The online enrollment counselor job is a customer-service position, not an academic position. I have seen some managers pass up candidates with extensive telephone and customer-service experience because they did not have a college degree, although they are willing to return to school to complete it. For me, these candidates represent a perfect choice. If I could convince them to enroll in one of my online degree-completion programs immediately, they would meet my skill requirements and know firsthand what it feels like to be an online student at my college.

After you have narrowed the field to a select few, you should conduct a telephone interview. You need to hear the candidates' voices and ask yourself the following questions:

- ☐ Are they friendly?
- ☐ Can I understand them clearly?
- ☐ Are they upbeat?
- ☐ Are they energetic?
- ☐ Do they know when to stop talking and listen?
- ☐ Can they let me explain the job duties without interrupting?
- ☐ Are they selling themselves too hard over the telephone?
- ☐ Did they hear what I told them?

When hiring enrollment counselors, I ask anyone who can pass a telephone interview to come in for a face-to-face interview.

Anyone who has hired an employee knows that during the face-to-face interview process, people usually hide their true selves. I like to use this time to give my candidates the good, the bad, and the ugly about the position. I already know what they are like on the telephone; now I get to see how they react when I tell them about a typical day in the life of an online enrollment counselor. I usually make the scenario as real as possible, covering everything from being hung up on 10 to 20 times a day to having their ears feel like they might bleed from talking on the telephone for 5 straight hours with one student who wants you to explain every page of your Web site. Some will smile, some will cringe, and some will simply say it is not the job for them.

Those who keep an open mind through all the horror stories and focus on the positive aspects of the job realize that this profession helps people make one of the most complicated and important decisions of their life—a decision that will change the destiny of their family for generations to come. I consider these candidates perfect for the job if they make it this far in the hiring process; are friendly and energetic; and have a positive outlook, a pleasant telephone voice, excellent listening skills, and an honest and heartfelt desire to help other people. I want these kinds of people on the telephone helping my students.

Training the Enrollment Counselor

The difference between poor enrollment counselors and exceptional ones lies in the quality of their training. Even at the University of Phoenix, the training I provided went above and beyond what the school expected, which resulted in the best trained and most productive enrollment counselors in the country—even though I did not choose my enrollment counselors based on their academic background, knowledge of the school, or past enrollment experience. As a result, I knew my counselors would require extensive training, which is nothing new in for-profit education. At many for-profit colleges, training consists of 1 to 2 weeks of classroom instruction before new counselors can start talking to prospective students on the telephone.

> At many for-profit colleges, training consists of 1 to 2 weeks of classroom instruction before new counselors can start talking to prospective students on the telephone.

The key topics of enrollment counselor training include the following:

- Higher education history and accreditation
- Institutional history
- Online program knowledge
- Admissions process
- Financial aid process
- Transfer credit process
- Online classroom knowledge
- Database management
- Phone etiquette
- Phone interviews and presentations
- Online competitors
- New-student orientation
- Retention

Only after I am satisfied that my counselors understand the basics of these topics will I allow them to make calls to students who requested information.

Training, however, must not end after the initial classroom sessions. It must continue and be consistent. Your online classroom serves as one of your most important training tools. Indeed, the best way to ensure consistent and ongoing training is to enroll your enrollment staff in an online class at your college. At a conference for online program administrators, I asked the group, "How many of you have ever taken an online class—either at your school or with another college?" I was shocked when only about 20% of the conference participants raised their hands. If you have never taken an online class, how can you possibly know what your students and staff are experiencing?

> If you have never taken an online class, how can you possibly know what your students and staff are experiencing?

Enrollment counselors who have taken online classes in the past, regardless of the institution they attended, add great value to your institution since they know how to relate to other online students. In my personal experience, previous or current online students usually make better online enrollment counselors. Therefore, if you do not offer free tuition for at least an introductory class to your enrollment counselors on the first day of their employment, you should. You cannot find a better training tool.

Chapter Summary

This chapter discussed the initial contact strategy for enrollment management and emphasized the enrollment counselor's role in initiating this personal contact strategy as a way to bond with prospective students. Staffing serves as the foundation of good online enrollment management and the key to enrollment success. Since the enrollment counselor plays the most vital role among staff members, any school absolutely must consider the nature of the enrollment counselor position, the steps for hiring counselors, the desired qualifications, and the importance of detailed training for new enrollment counselors.

Chapter Three

An Average
Day

This chapter covers the following **key points**:

» Enrollment counselor work environment

» Average day for an enrollment counselor

- Review the day's activities

- Contact recent leads

- Call database contacts

- Prepare for telephone appointments

- Conduct telephone interviews and application walk-through

The average day for an online enrollment counselor varies depending on the day of the week. Most online counselors are hired with the expectation that they will work Monday through Friday and occasionally on Saturday, anywhere between 9 a.m. and 8 p.m. Each counselor works the late shift, usually 11 a.m. to 8 p.m., 2 days during the week. The other 3 days of the week, he or she works 9 a.m. to 6 p.m.

Each counselor has a workstation cubicle rather than an office, as online enrollment takes place over the telephone and the Internet. A cubicle arrangement allows managers to more effectively supervise and train their staff because they can hear the counselors and answer any questions immediately. The issue of privacy arose one day when a campus enrollment manager told me that his staff members would never work in cubicles because it diminishes their right to privacy. My response was simple: Enrollment counselors are employed to service students, and good service requires constant and immediate support. If counselors cannot answer a student's question, they have a responsibility to find the answer as quickly as possible. In a cubicle environment, counselors can simply raise their hand or stand up and ask another counselor for the answer. This is a fast-paced, nonstop service position, and you need to manage it as such. Remember, the average student will request information from at least five schools, therefore speed of contact and urgency of response will separate successful online programs from failed ones.

> Enrollment counselors are employed to service students, and good service requires constant and immediate support.

> Speed of contact and urgency of response will separate successful online programs from failed ones.

The following example shows a day in the life of a successful online enrollment counselor.

The Day Begins

Step 1

Review the day's planned activities.

Jill works as an enrollment counselor at your campus. She arrives at 10:45 a.m. on Monday morning because she is working one of her two late shifts for the week. She gets her coffee, says hello to the rest of the staff, and meets with her manager to discuss the day's planned activities and any issues that may have arisen during the previous day. This meeting lasts anywhere from a few minutes to a half hour, depending on the day and the issues they need to cover.

It is January 5, and your college has a term starting on March 5. The previous summer, Jill's manager gave her a goal of enrolling 20 new students for the March term. She has an enrollment goal for every term and, because she has known her goals since last summer and knows her own conversions, she knows exactly how to achieve them.

After meeting with her manager, Jill returns to her desk just before 11 a.m. and is ready to start the day. She looks at her schedule for the day and sees that she has a telephone interview (3 p.m.), a classroom demonstration walk-through (6:30 p.m.), and an application walk-through (7 p.m.). Since her first telephone appointment will not take place until 3 p.m., she knows that she needs to call people in her database from 11 a.m. until she takes her lunch in the afternoon. She knows that from 3 p.m. until 8 p.m. she will most likely remain busy with back-to-back appointments. During these next few hours, she will have her only opportunity to call leads and set up activities for tomorrow.

Every request for information represents a lead, and Jill has nearly 500 leads in her database going back 18 months. She also has an additional 500 recycled leads going back 3 years. She uses lead creation dates to group the leads so that she can call the leads efficiently and provide the appropriate voice mail message, e-mail, and marketing tool. She has grouped her leads as follows: less than 48 hours old (hot), 48 hours to 1 week (warm), 1 week to 3 months, 3 months to 6 months, 6 months to 12 months, more than 12 months, and recycled.

Less than 48 hours old (hot)

48 hours to 1 week (warm)

1 week to 3 months

3 months to 6 months

6 months to 12 months

More than 12 months

Recycled Leads

Jill knows that speed matters greatly and that her first priority is to contact the most recent leads in her database. Four leads came in over the weekend, but she still has 12 from last week that she has not been able to contact. She immediately calls the four newest leads and reaches one potential student. The conversation lasts for only a few moments because the prospect is on his way to work; however, Jill schedules a telephone appointment with the prospect for tomorrow afternoon.

She then begins to call her leads from last week but the only person she reaches is one who is no longer interested and wants to be removed from Jill's contact list. To prevent Jill or another representative from making further contact, Jill makes the necessary changes in her database. Now that she has finished calling her most recent leads, Jill is actually pleased that in less than an hour, she has called all of her priority leads and set up an appointment. She plans to contact the three remaining leads from the weekend later in the afternoon, and she sets to work calling the older leads in her database.

Step 2

Contact recent leads.

Many of the people who request information from her school are just "shopping" colleges. Jill knows that many of the other colleges her leads are shopping will not give them the service they need. As a result, many potential students will give up on the idea of returning to school. Jill resolves to find those students in her database, and she begins calling her old leads.

Step 3

Call database contacts.

As the day progresses, she successfully contacts four more potential students, three of whom come from leads created at least 6 months ago. In each case, the prospective student had to put college on hold for some reason, such as settling into a new job, starting a family, or feeling overwhelmed at the time of the original inquiry. Since then, circumstances in their lives have changed, and two of them are ready to go back to college.

Jill has placed 50 calls in 2½ hours, made six contacts, and set three more appointments for an application walk-through and information meeting. Jill changes the status of each contact in her database and schedules her new appointments. It is now 1:30 p.m. and time for lunch.

The Day Ends

Step 4

Prepare for telephone appointments.

At 2:30 p.m., Jill returns from lunch and begins to prepare for a 3 p.m. telephone interview with a prospect. She first opens and then minimizes the college's Web site on her computer screen. Since the prospect had requested information about the school's bachelor's degree program in criminal justice, Jill loads the information sheet about the program and prepares to send it by e-mail as soon as she begins her telephone meeting. She is prepared, confident, and ready to go.

Jill notices, however, that the message light is flashing on her telephone. In the rush to prepare for her appointment, she forgot to check her messages, including one from her 3 p.m. prospect. He has cancelled and wants to reschedule the telephone interview. Jill immediately calls him back on his cell phone but reaches his voice mail. She knows that leaving a message and asking someone to call back means that she cannot call that person again until that person has had enough time to return the call. Jill decides not to leave a message and makes a note to call again in an hour.

Since the prospect cancelled his appointment, Jill knows that she must now get back on the telephone and keep calling old leads, always looking for that one student who needs a little help and encouragement. Over the next 2 hours, she calls 40 old leads, and her persistence pays off. She finds a student who had requested information last year but decided to attend the local community college and never informed Jill of his decision. A year later, he left the community college. He felt frustrated with the entire experience and believed that the community college staff viewed him as just another number and never gave him the support he needed. Since leaving the community college, he has accepted a full-time job and become a father. As much as he wants to finish his degree, he knows the additional time commitments of job and family mean his dreams of college will have to wait.

> **Step 5**
>
> Conduct phone interviews and application walk-throughs.

> He felt frustrated with the entire experience and believed that the community college staff viewed him as just another number and never gave him the support he needed.

Jill knows the strengths of her college and that she can help him. She spends the next hour talking to the prospect, getting to know him and what he needs from a college in order to succeed. Jill asks him to access the college's Web site. She is familiar with every page of the site and knows the location of every piece of information. She covers all of the course material, program details, tuition costs, financial aid, and online classroom requirements. Within an hour, the prospect excitedly asks to complete an application.

Jill has done her job. She never gave up on the potential students in her database, understanding that every name in her database represents someone who may need her help. She knows that she is the one advantage her school has that no other school will ever have. She cares more, tries harder, and helps more than any other enrollment counselor at any other college. The new student probably requested information from several schools the same day that Jill received his information more than a year ago, but everyone else gave up on him. Jill earned her pay today. It is now 8 p.m., and she has made eight contacts, set four appointments, and picked up an application. She turns off her computer and the lights and goes home knowing she just changed a life.

Chapter Summary

This chapter captured an average day in the life of an enrollment counselor. It also discussed work-space configuration and recommended that enrollment counselors use workstation cubicles to foster a supportive team environment that enables enrollment managers to more effectively supervise the counselors who are giving support to prospective students. This chapter further reviewed how an enrollment counselor might schedule and arrange a day's activities, call recent leads, contact leads from a database, and conduct telephone appointments and an application walk-through for interested prospects. This hypothetical day serves as just one example of how enrollment counselors might structure a workday. At the same time, the example illustrates how to manage an enrollment division effectively.

Chapter Four

From Lead to Enrollment

This chapter covers the following **key points**:

- » The lead management process
- » Lead creation and tracking
- » Controlling the conversation with the lead
- » Giving information to the lead
- » Managing the application process
- » The importance of acceptance
- » The post-acceptance black hole

I took my first job in college enrollment management 14 years ago. All of the enrollment counselors had on their desks a long, wooden box filled with index cards. It reminded me of a card-catalog file found at libraries in years past. Each card contained a prospective student's handwritten name, phone number, and any additional information he or she provided. Each counselor sorted the cards according to date and month and developed a system for calling the leads. Most leads came from the college's three high-school presenters who visited all of the local schools within 50 miles of the college in an effort to find as many names and telephone numbers of college-bound seniors as possible. By the end of the year, each presenter would have at least 3,000 names and telephone numbers. I had a staff of five enrollment counselors who called each name during the course of the year. The counselors took notes on each person's index card. If a counselor left the college, the replacement counselor received the former employee's box of leads. Once a year, the counselors would go through the lead boxes, remove the least-promising leads, and place them into a box known as the orphanage. As the college expanded and hired additional staff, each new employee worked with the orphans until he or she accumulated enough new leads.

Today, lead management is a sophisticated science with specific results arising from specific actions. Computer-generated lead rotations, lead recycling, auto-generated e-mail blasts, and text messaging have dramatically changed the way enrollment counselors contact students who request information. However, good, old-fashioned, voice-to-voice contact has not changed. It has no substitute. The old enrollment principle—those who bond will win—has never been more alive than in today's online education market.

> The old enrollment principle—those who bond will win—has never been more alive than in today's online education market.

Online education is impersonal in many ways. When students request information over the Internet, they have no idea who will contact them or when. They have no bond with the college and no reason to exhibit loyalty. Since they have not visited the campus, they know nothing about the beautiful landscaping or the incredible new science laboratory made possible with donations from wealthy alumni. They see the school's Web site, name, programs, and tuition cost, and that is the extent of their familiarity with the school. Maybe they had a friend or relative who attended the college years ago and shared positive information about the school. Or maybe they searched online for all of the local colleges that offered online programs, and your college appeared first in the list of search results. How they found you does not really matter. It only matters that they requested information. Now what?

> Online education is impersonal in many ways.

Lead Creation

Where do you generate most of your leads? Do they come from your Web site? Do they come from student referrals, alumni, or college-fair presenters? Whatever the source of your leads, you are probably adding them to your lead database. At many colleges, the database often becomes a bottomless pit where leads enter but soon disappear forever.

> At many colleges, the database often becomes a bottomless pit where leads enter but soon disappear forever.

I cannot give specific examples on how to best capture and manage your information requests, but dozens of computer systems adequately perform these tasks. Most colleges have their own beloved system in place for this purpose. However, I can give you a for-profit example of how you can capture, distribute, manage, and convert leads into enrollments. It is the principles of speed and urgency that matter, not the ability to recreate a system the size of the University of Phoenix.

All institutions have a similar basic process for capturing and managing leads. Students visit your Web site and explore online program information. Let's assume they like what they see. At this point, the differences between for-profit online colleges and non-profit online colleges become clear. On a for-profit college's Web site, students click on a link to request information and complete an online form. From there, two options exist, depending on the size of the for-profit online college. At a large online college such as the University of Phoenix, the system sends the information to a call center within a split second of the request for information. At a smaller for-profit online college, the system sends the request directly to a lead manager working on the campus. This person could be an admissions assistant, a manager, or a marketing specialist. Regardless of the person's position, only one person distributes the leads.

In the call center example, the lead instantly goes to a call center representative who reviews the information and calls the lead immediately. If the student does not answer, the representative attempts to contact the student multiple times over the next several days until the lead is eventually transferred to a local enrollment counselor's database. If the call center representative successfully contacts the student, then he or she verifies the lead's name, telephone number, and e-mail address listed on the request-for-information form. The representative may then verify that the student has a high school diploma or a GED, resides in the United States, and has in mind a program of interest.

After asking a few basic questions, the representative transfers the student to the enrollment team assigned to that person's ZIP code, state, or regional territory. As soon as a lead is created for a large college, the information is automatically uploaded into the campus customer-relationship management system and assigned an identification number. This prevents duplication of effort and allows enrollment counselors to see the student's information the minute they receive the transferred call.

Small for-profit colleges have a less efficient but still highly effective process for managing their leads. The system sends the lead to an assigned lead manager via e-mail, and the lead manager immediately enters the lead information into the database and assigns the lead to a specific enrollment counselor on campus. The counselor receives an e-mail, and a call task is assigned in the system. At a well-managed college, this immediate need takes priority over all other aspects of the lead manager's job. Speed is crucial, and the clock is now ticking. Once the counselor successfully contacts the student, both the direct and the indirect lead-handling processes flow in a similar fashion.

> Once the counselor successfully contacts the student, both the direct and the indirect lead-handling processes flow in a similar fashion.

 Controlling the Conversation with the Lead

When talking to the student on the telephone, the enrollment counselor's main objective is to control the conversation. Prospective students have many questions, and a good enrollment counselor knows that to give students the correct information, he or she must find out more details about the students' needs. Reciting information from a script does not help students or produce results since every lead has different needs. Most students have no idea what questions to ask when they first speak to an enrollment counselor. Most believe that they just need to know the length of the program, the tuition cost, and the financial aid process. However, so much more goes into making a good decision about which educational institution to select.

To gain and maintain control of the conversation, the enrollment counselor must spend a few minutes chatting informally with the student until the student begins to relax and understand that the enrollment counselor is there to help. When the student has relaxed, the counselor begins to ask a series of questions about the student's educational background, current employment, plans for the future, and financing arrangements. We will cover this topic in greater detail in a later chapter.

 Questions that Guide the Conversation

Enrollment counselors need to ask the following questions to guide the conversation with the student:

- What is your educational background? Have you obtained a degree or taken any college courses?
- Are you currently employed? What is your occupation?
- What are your future plans? Why are you interested in going back to school now?
- How do you plan to pay for your education? Are you interested in receiving information about financial aid?

The success of the interview process depends on how well the enrollment counselor convinces the student to answer each set of questions. The student's answers allow the enrollment counselor to select which features and benefits to discuss later in the interview. Remember, every student has different wants and needs. The more the counselor uncovers about the student's motivation, the better the counselor can serve the student. Always remember the 80/20 rule, which states that a good counselor should listen at least 80% of the time and talk 20% of the time. The enrollment counselor must focus on the student, working to uncover the student's specific wants and needs. Remember, those who bond will win.

Giving Information

After the enrollment counselor prompts the student with questions about the student's needs, the conversation can move in several different directions. The following three scenarios might unfold:

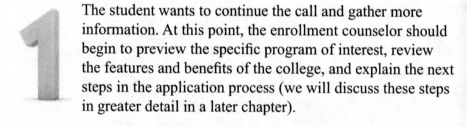

The student wants to continue the call and gather more information. At this point, the enrollment counselor should begin to preview the specific program of interest, review the features and benefits of the college, and explain the next steps in the application process (we will discuss these steps in greater detail in a later chapter).

The student wants to review the information and continue the conversation later. In this case, the enrollment counselor should try to schedule a telephone appointment within the next 24-48 hours. Remember, speed matters greatly. The student probably requested information from several colleges, and these other schools will also attempt to contact the student soon.

The student wants to review the information and does not want to set a future appointment. In this case, the enrollment counselor should make a note in the database to attempt a follow-up call approximately 3-4 days after the initial conversation.

If the student chooses option 1, the enrollment counselor

ends the process of acquiring information and begins delivering information. He or she must do this in a deliberate sequence. A good enrollment counselor will learn a great deal of information during the initial call and can select the specific features and benefits of the school that will interest the student.

Not everyone agrees with this approach. A non-profit college enrollment manager told me that this process was "sleazy," "slick," and "unethical." My first question was, "Why?" She began a lengthy lecture explaining that convincing students to speak openly and share their fears, wants, needs, and hopes for the future and then tailoring a presentation to meet those issues is just wrong. So I asked, "Why is it wrong?" She rolled her eyes and stepped away from the conversation.

In my opinion, it is not wrong to listen to a student, let the student share his or her needs, and then provide the information to address those individual needs. It is not wrong; it is simply providing good service.

The Application

Assume that the student wants to proceed with the online application process. Do you send the student the link to the application and let the student complete it without any assistance? If your answer is "yes," then I must ask you the following question: Do you know that many students begin filling out a college application but do not submit it? In fact, 40 to 50% of students who begin an online application never complete it or submit it. The answer to my original question should be a resounding "no."

During a presentation to non-profit college administrators, I mentioned this same issue. One person said, "If they cannot complete the application, then we probably do not want them as students." Most students who begin your college application process probably have some interest in your college, so why would you not try to help them? Most students who stop completing an application do so at a point where the application asks for information that they do not have readily available. I once saw an online application that had a mandatory field for the address of the student's high school. If you did not know it, you could not proceed with the application. Most people probably do not know the physical address of their high school, so why would a college make it a mandatory field in their application?

> Most students who stop completing an application do so at a point where the application asks for information that they do not have readily available.

When students run into these roadblocks, they save and close the application and plan to return to it after they find the missing information. Do you remember how many schools a student will shop online? Do you realize how many colleges have an easy, fast, and user-friendly application? If you believe that you will not lose that student to an enrollment counselor from a for-profit college who will stay on the line and walk the student through every possible application obstacle, you are sadly mistaken. If a for-profit enrollment counselor contacts the student 5 minutes after the student leaves your online application uncompleted, the for-profit counselor will surely help the student complete his or her online application. They do this with a simple statement: "I will stay with you while you complete the application, and I will be here to help you every step of the way." After all, those who bond will win.

Getting Accepted

In the United States, a huge misconception surrounds the issue of for-profit college acceptance rates versus non-profit college acceptance rates. According to the U.S. Department of Education, both types of 4-year institutions have similar acceptance rates: 57% for the 4-year, for-profit colleges and 51% for the 4-year, private, non-profit colleges (U.S. Department of Education, 2007). The most significant difference involves the speed at which for-profit colleges accept students. This constitutes a serious issue because the sooner you can accept a student, the sooner the student will commit to your college. A typical for-profit college will process and accept students within 1-2 weeks. Many non-profit colleges, however, take 1-2 months—or longer—to accept students. With every day that passes, the student remains vulnerable to your competitors and uncommitted to your institution.

> The associate dean of enrollment at a non-profit college once told me that it was "unethical" to contact a student who had applied to another college and that his school would never do this. I asked him if he meant it was unethical to recruit a student who had been accepted or that it was unethical to recruit a student who simply had applied to another college. He answered, "I believe it is unethical once the student has applied."

If you call a student who has requested information from your school and you discover that the student applied to Jones College but has not received an acceptance notice, do you apologize for the call, wish the student luck at Jones College, and then hang up the telephone? Or do you stay on the telephone and try to discover what the student really needs in a college? Perhaps your college and your online structure would provide a better fit for the student.

If you believe that the only ethical answer involves hanging up and never contacting the student again, you have not really made an ethical decision; your decision means you neglected your obligation as a senior manager to protect the best interests of your students and the financial well-being of your institution. A college that rests its hopes on the anticipated courteous behavior of another college will lose every time. A huge gap exists between being a hard-working, aggressive enrollment counselor and being an unethical enrollment counselor.

The Black Hole

> For many non-profit colleges, an enormous black hole exists between a student's acceptance into the school and the student starting classes.

For many non-profit colleges, an enormous black hole exists between a student's acceptance into the school and the student starting classes. The average 4-year, private, non-profit college has an accepted-to-enrollment conversion rate of 31%. However, the average 4-year, for-profit college has a conversion rate of 79% (U.S. Department of Education, 2007). The difference is significant.

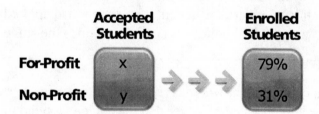

What accounts for this dramatic gap? Three reasons come to mind:

 Length of time between acceptance and the start of classes

For-profit colleges know that students are vulnerable and often will allow unreasonable fears and low self-confidence to change their decision about attending a particular college. The University of Phoenix, for example, allows students to start classes every week. Most colleges, of course, cannot do this but it is possible to increase your program entry points to decrease the gap as much as possible. The speed of acceptance is critical. Non-profit colleges that only start new classes quarterly often make students wait months to start a program after they have been accepted. Every day, week, and month that passes between application and the start date of classes means more lost enrollments.

Financial aid

Another reason for the disparity in conversion rates involves the psychological impact of being financially cleared to start class. The more quickly a school can determine a student's financial aid package, the more comfortable that student will feel about starting classes at the college. The financial aid process represents one of the most frustrating and disillusioning aspects of starting college. Once students complete the financial aid process with one school, they do not usually change their mind about which school they want to attend. The last ordeal students want to experience again is the financial aid process. At many for-profit colleges, the school and the student complete the financial aid process within just a few days of the student's acceptance. This represents yet another reason why you should keep your financial aid department fully staffed at all times.

> The more quickly a school can determine a student's financial aid package, the more comfortable that student will feel about starting classes at the college.

Post-acceptance follow-up

The disparity in conversion rates is also related to how much post-acceptance follow-up a school provides to students. At for-profit institutions, enrollment counselors know that a student's struggle to attend college does not end with acceptance. Accepted students probably have shopped several other schools and will continue to receive marketing literature by postal mail or e-mail from other schools. A shiny new toy in the window can turn many heads. For-profit enrollment managers understand this and always encourage their enrollment staff to contact students weekly until the students start classes. Many for-profit colleges have gone so far as to develop application-retention strategies for every new applicant. Most non-profit college administrators believe that after acceptance, the responsibility for moving forward lies in the students' hands. The difference in mindset between for-profit colleges and non-profit colleges explains the difference in start rates.

Chapter Summary

This chapter examined the lead management process from finding leads to enrolling students. It provided a for-profit model of lead generation and management so that non-profit colleges can apply similar principles to their institutions. This model routes leads from their generation to either a call center or a lead manager who can contact the leads directly or distribute the leads to an enrollment counselor's database for follow-up. This chapter also focused on a successful model's key actions, exploring how the enrollment counselor can control the conversation with the student, give the student the needed information, and direct the application process. The chapter also covered the importance of the rate of acceptance for students and how enrollment counselors can manage the black hole of time that occurs after the school has accepted the students.

Chapter Five

The Online Interview

This chapter covers the following **key points**:

- » Purpose for the student interview
- » Features and benefits discussed during the interview
- » Structure of the interview
- » Questions to ask the student
- » How to discuss financial options and pricing with the student
- » Closing the interview with an application

The topic of converting prospects into applications arose once during a conversation with a college president. He was concerned about the way in which his staff had been handling the enrollment process. He told me that his school required every student to participate in a face-to-face interview on campus prior to acceptance. I asked him if he applied this policy to his online programs, and he responded, "Of course I do." He said that an interview had always served as part of the acceptance policy and that even online students need to get a "feel for the college" to make a good decision. His main concern was that while his school received many online applications, few applicants came for their interview. As a result, he had to reject the applications.

Unfortunately, this college administrator is not the only one who strongly believes in a mandatory face-to-face interview. I have met several others who have the same policy for their online students. I have also heard many non-profit administrators say that if students want a degree from a particular college, they should at least have to step foot on the campus.

Remember that online students value *convenience*. Is it convenient to require students who live 50 miles away to drive to campus for an interview when a dozen other online colleges with the same programs do not? Do you think these students will reject your college because of this policy? They absolutely will.

> Remember that online students value convenience.

Many administrators believe that the college interview works to weed out undesirable students. Administrators who believe this is the purpose of a college interview and

> Students have changed, the competition has changed, and the purpose of the college interview has changed.

think they can apply this notion to their online programs have made a huge mistake. Students have changed, the competition has changed, and the purpose of the college interview has changed. In the world of online enrollment, the heart of the interview is value. The school will find the interview valuable, but the student must as well.

Value

Value changes constantly. Every individual views it differently, and it almost always changes over time. For the online enrollment interview, I define the term *value* as the current level of exchange: The more I can get right now for what I have to give right now, the more valuable I will find it right now. So, how is an online college interview valuable to the school and to the student? Look to the for-profit colleges for the answer. I can assure you that they take the online student interview quite seriously—but not for the reason you might expect.

At a for-profit college, the opportunity to discover the student's true wants and needs and whether the college's programs can meet those needs develops during the student interview. Enrollment counselors delve into the student's prior educational experience and admissibility, gauge which features and benefits to explore with the student, and discover whether the student has the time and the money necessary to complete the degree coursework. The world of online education is impersonal and remote, so the interview may serve as your only chance to get to know and bond with each student, overcome each student's objections, and discover obstacles in the path to success. At for-profit colleges, the interview represents the most valuable step in the acceptance process.

As for students, the interview represents an opportunity for them to ask questions about the program and learn about the online structure of the college, the cost of tuition and fees, how to apply for financial aid, and how the application process works, including its requirements and time frame. You can cover all of this information in the course of an hour-long interview. Is the interview valuable to the student? It is—without a doubt.

Features and Benefits

If you ask online enrollment managers, "What is the most important aspect of an online student interview," most of them will tell you to discover early in the conversation which features and benefits matter most to students. This leads me to ask, "What are features and benefits, and why are they so important to a for-profit enrollment team?" Before I answer, let me ask another question first: "How short is your attention span?" Imagine walking into a restaurant with the sole intention of ordering a steak. You sit down at your table, and the waiter proceeds to tell you about every dish on the menu—not just the dinner menu, but also the breakfast menu, the lunch menu and even the early bird specials from last Tuesday. How long will it take before you lose patience and feel frustrated? Not long, I suspect. Uncovering specific needs and addressing them quickly is one of the key differences between for-profit and non-profit college interviews.

> Uncovering specific needs and addressing them quickly is one of the key differences between for-profit and non-profit college interviews.

You do not interview online students to talk about your college's great lacrosse team or all of the famous alumni who may have attended back in the 1940s. You want to get to know the student and the student's wants and needs. If you understand which features and benefits of your college apply to a particular student's situation, you can build value throughout the interview.

The information you learn from the student during the interview helps you decide which of your college's features and benefits will interest the student. Features are facts about your college. For example, your college is regionally accredited, it has a liberal transfer policy, it has reasonable tuition rates, and it has an excellent reputation with local employers. As an online counselor, you should maintain a list of at least 20 features related to your college that you have ingrained in your memory since your initial training.

> As an online counselor, you should maintain a list of at least 20 features related to your college that you have ingrained in your memory since your initial training.

Benefits stem from features. Most enrollment counselors can easily see the benefits of a feature, but students are not experts. Never assume that a student will know the benefits. Your counselors need to make sure they present them at all times. For example: Jones College has a great reputation with local employers (feature). Having an MBA from Jones College may carry a lot more weight on your resume than an MBA from a large, for-profit college (benefit). As an education professional, it may sound obvious to you, but never assume.

> The key to a successful interview is your ability to know which features and benefits to highlight and when to discuss them with the student.

You can create and choose from literally hundreds of different combinations of features and benefits. The key to a successful interview is your ability to know which features and benefits to highlight and when to discuss them with the student. Remember that a student interview conducted over the telephone is not a give-and-take exercise; it is a take-and-give exercise. You must first ask questions so you can take information from the student; only then can you honestly give the student the specific information the student seeks.

The Structure

Each for-profit college uses its own names or acronyms for the 10 interview steps listed below. The order of the steps may vary, but the interview usually has a similar basic structure:

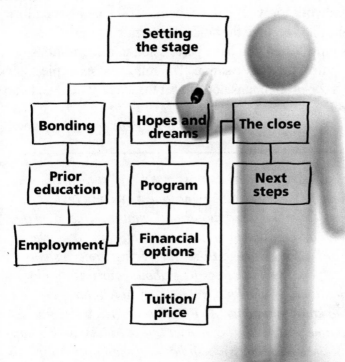

In a student interview with a for-profit college, the interview focuses on mutual value. First you take information (from the student), and then you give information (to the student). The ability to control the conversation determines the interview's success, and most for-profit counselors undergo training on this 10-step method from their first day on the job. Most will master the skill after a few months of practice. During all stages of the interview process, counselors are taught to take detailed notes about the questions asked and the answers received.

Doing this will help them better respond to the student's needs.

1 Setting the Stage

This step has a twofold value: In it, you will lay the groundwork for what will happen over the next several minutes and receive the student's permission to ask questions. When you have permission to ask questions, you can control the conversation. The following example shows how a for-profit counselor can set the stage for a telephone interview:

OK, John, I am sure you have many questions; every new student does. Today, I want to make sure we cover all of your questions and review the online program, tuition, financial aid options, and what it is like to be an online student. I was an online student myself, and I am sure you have the same questions I did when I started. First, I am going to need some basic information from you. I will ask questions about your prior college experience, your educational goals, how much time you will have for college, and just get to know you better. As I promised when we set the appointment on the phone yesterday, the interview should take only about an hour. By the time we are finished, you will have all the information you need to make a good decision. So, let's get started. . . .

I have heard this done a hundred different ways over the years, but once you know the basics, you can develop an opening that matches your style. When a counselor uses an opening like this one during an interview, the student will usually wait until later to ask questions and let you do your job of gathering information. You might be surprised at how much information a student wants to give you if you only set the stage and help the student feel comfortable.

2 Bonding

The need to bond with prospective students drives many large for-profit colleges to plant their campus flags within a 50-mile radius of a large media market. Nothing can replace the local touch; small independent colleges should take heed and use the strategy to their advantage. On many occasions, I have walked past the cubicles of my enrollment counselors only to find them talking with a student on the telephone about the local high school football scores, where they shop for clothes, or where they can find a great sushi restaurant.

> Nothing can replace the local touch; small independent colleges should take heed and use the strategy to their advantage.

These counselors are doing their job. They are bonding with online students who probably would have felt like invisible names and numbers had they spoken to a representative at any other college—assuming they actually had a chance to speak to a person at all. If you hire people who care, are friendly, and love to talk on the telephone, you will reap your rewards.

3 Prior Education

Eventually, all the small talk must end as you shift the focus of the interview to the student's enrollment. You need to ask questions about the student's prior educational experience. Most online students have attended at least one prior college class even if they earned no credits. This stage of the interview process matters greatly for several reasons; however, this stage will not give you a sense of how the person will perform as a student in the future. That is not the point. A past failure at the local community college does not indicate a future success or failure. You want to know what the student liked and did not like about

> **The best question you can ask an online transfer student is, "Why did you decide to leave your previous college?"**

the prior college. The best question you can ask an online transfer student is, "Why did you decide to leave your previous college?" I once had a student talk for 20 minutes after I asked that question, and the initial answer led to additional questions. By the time he had finished talking, he had given me all of the information I needed to know. Let the student talk. Remember, you are building a list of features and benefits to use later in the interview.

4 Employment

Most online students work either full-time or part-time jobs. During this stage of the interview process, students will tell you about the importance of convenience. You can also learn other important information during this stage such as their current work schedule and future plans for advancement. Probe for answers with questions such as the following: Do you have time for an online class? Do you dislike your job and dream of a day when you will find something better? Do you want to move up in your current position? Does your employer offer tuition reimbursement? The answers to each of these questions will lead you to a specific feature and benefit to highlight when you start talking about the college and the online programs it offers.

5 Hopes and Dreams

What hopes and dreams does the student have for the future? If you have not learned the answer already, now is the perfect time to ask one of the most basic and important of all interview questions: "Why do you want to go back to school?" Or you can ask, "What will this degree do for you and your family?"

At this point in the interview process, you have been talking with the student for maybe half an hour, and the student has answered many questions. You probably have bonded with the student, and the student is willing to speak openly. Now you are looking for a serious reason why the student wants to return to college and finish an interrupted degree. This is not the time to accept a one- or two-sentence answer. You want the *real* reason. Prod the student to think seriously and thoughtfully about the answer. Today may be the first time the student has said the reason out loud to anyone. The reason becomes the student's reality through this process. If you reinforce that reality through active listening, the student can truly understand their own desire to go back to college.

The Program   6

At this point in the interview process, you have asked all of the appropriate questions, received all of the student's answers, and decided on at least a half-dozen features and benefits that will help the student. Now you must transition from taking information to giving information.

One of the most important tools a good online counselor can use at this stage is the computer—yours and the student's. Tell the student to sit in front of a computer and follow along as you expertly navigate around your college's Web site. Most online schools maintain an electronic version of their online program information flyers; often, however, counselors will present this information to students directly from the college's Web site.

During earlier stages of the interview, you probably learned why the student selected a particular program to study. For example, if the student said that he or she wanted to pursue a criminal justice degree because it provides opportunities to work in juvenile corrections, you can immediately highlight the Introduction to Juvenile Justice and Juvenile Criminal Procedures courses that serve as part of the college's criminal justice program. Have the course descriptions readily available, and review the information with the student.

Now you can begin to cover the questions that most new online students ask, including the following: What is it like taking an online class? How will I attend class? What if I need help? Here is where having a counselor with an online student background can help. The experiences of all online students involve virtually the same issues, regardless of the college or online format. I, for example, found myself completely lost in the University of Phoenix's online library—to the point where I had to contact the online librarian for help—and I was the director of enrollment. The point is that no substitute exists for the online student experience. We all had the same fears, and we all had the same questions when we started. You need to let the student know that you will be there to help when classes start and that all students have the same fears. These reassuring words help build an essential bond between the enrollment counselor and student.

> You need to let the student know that you will be there to help when classes start and that all students have the same fears. These reassuring words help build an essential bond between the enrollment counselor and student.

7 Financial Options

With the student now excited about the program, you move on to address in detail the issues of tuition and financing options. I have heard tuition discussed a dozen different ways on a dozen different campuses. Some colleges quote a price per credit hour, others per term, and still others per academic year. One of the worst mistakes you can make as an enrollment counselor is to quote a tuition price in any manner, and then leave the subject completely.

You need to reassure students that most online students can attend college if they apply for financial aid and that such aid is available if they qualify. Indeed, you should be able to say that one of the great features of your college is that the financial aid staff members are friendly and helpful (feature) and available to assist new students with the process (benefit). One note of caution: If you plan to tell students about financial aid, make sure your college's financial aid office has the appropriate staffing to meet the expectations you create.

> If you plan to tell students about financial aid, make sure your college's financial aid office has the appropriate staffing to meet the expectations you create.

Tuition/Price

8

Astute enrollment counselors know the tuition costs of their competitors. If they have done their research, they will have discovered that most for-profit colleges charge considerably more than most non-profit colleges when it comes to tuition for their online programs. Counselors need to understand that if price truly were an issue, then for-profit colleges could not charge $400-$600 per credit hour for an online degree and still have hundreds of thousands of students.

For-profit enrollment counselors know that the cost of tuition is not the issue; rather, the issue is the value of the service. Most students would rather pay a little more and get personalized help and attention than pay a little less and feel completely on their own throughout the enrollment process. Just imagine the success a non-profit college could realize with lower tuition and incredible personalized attention. The college would dominate its market.

9 The Close

The next step is to seal the deal. It might seem bizarre, but I have seen enrollment counselors conduct a 1-hour telephone interview, talk to an excited student on the other end of the line, and still feel afraid to ask the student to complete an application. I have seen this happen at every for-profit and non-profit college I have visited. People who care about other people want to appear helpful, not pushy; ultimately, however, the time comes when you must ask the question.

The ability to close is the most difficult skill for enrollment counselors to master. Many of them never perform the task well no matter how hard they try. To get around this roadblock, many for-profit colleges instruct their staff members to skip the question entirely and say to the student, "While I have you on the phone, let's just go ahead and get your application started." If you have done your job well up to this point, such a statement rarely raises an issue, because you will know if the student is serious based on the cues you picked up during the interview. Regardless of how you persuade the student to begin completing the application, you absolutely must stay on the telephone with the student while the student completes the form.

> You absolutely must stay on the telephone with the student while the student completes the form.

As mentioned earlier, many students will begin a college application online but never complete it. They may plan to return later and finish the task, but many times they never come back. You need to let the student know that the application process is not difficult, the application will take only a few minutes to complete, and you will be here to help. For example, if the student encounters a puzzling item on the application (such as the address of the student's high school or the specific day and month the student left another college), you can advise the student about what really matters and what he or she can correct later. The goal is a complete and submitted application.

Next Steps

But don't stop yet. Enrollment counselors make a mistake if they let the student end the call before they explain the next steps in the application process. At this point, you want to cover important dates and deadlines for receiving additional documentation, such as transcripts, recommendations, and test scores and helping them complete their financial aid applications.

If you have access to the schedules of staff members in the college's financial aid office, ask the student if he or she can set aside time in the next few days to speak to a representative. Many colleges lose applicants simply because they fail to give financial aid the full attention it deserves. If your college's financial aid office does not have the proper staffing and you cannot schedule a voice-to-voice appointment with a financial aid officer now, then you may lose a nervous student.

Even if you clear the financial aid hurdle, you can still lose students for other reasons. Many colleges require students to request their transcripts from previous colleges on their own, rather than requesting them for the student. If this is the case at your college, verify that your counselors have a firm, efficient follow-up plan in place. You cannot simply say, "We will let you know when your transcripts arrive." You should instead set a date for a follow-up telephone call to the student to verify that the student has ordered

> Many colleges require students to request their transcripts from previous colleges on their own, rather than requesting them for the student. If this is the case at your college, verify that your counselors have a firm, efficient follow-up plan in place.

the transcripts. You could also use a notification system to alert counselors when a student's transcripts have arrived at the college. Many colleges use automatically generated e-mail to notify assigned counselors when transcripts have been scanned into the college's computer system.

More important than just having a system in place, however, is having a system that functions properly. Nothing is more frustrating than losing students who are truly interested in enrolling but feel like the college bureaucracy is giving them the runaround. You need to know how all your enrollment processes work. Just a few tweaks to the process can save you from losing dozens of applicants every year.

Chapter Summary

This chapter examined the interview process for enrolling prospective online students. In an online enrollment environment, the interview needs to be valuable to the student and should provide the student with desired and pertinent information, including the features and benefits of the college and program information. The chapter also covered the basic structure of a telephone interview and the prompting questions that enrollment counselors need to ask during the interview to elicit relevant information from the student. The chapter then discussed how to give students the information they need to feel comfortable with their decisions. Finally, the chapter presented some guidelines for closing the interview with a completed application and for covering the next steps in the process with the student.

Chapter Six

Conversion Management

This chapter covers the following **key points**:

- » Distinguishing between types of conversion
- » Importance of multiple types of conversion
- » Description and management of seven basic conversions:
  - Lead to contact
  - Contact to activity
  - Activity to application
  - Application to accepted
  - Accepted to new start
  - Lead to new start
  - Application to new start

The ability to manage leads, staff members, and student enrollments through the interpretation of conversions represents one of the most important skills that online directors of enrollment need to master. The interpretation of conversions is also one of the most complex and misunderstood areas of modern enrollment management. The problem is twofold: Fallible human beings are responsible for interpreting conversion data, and interpretations vary according to college policy and managers' experiences. The way I interpret data and the way another manager interprets data may differ altogether. I have been fortunate, however, in that I have forecasted fairly accurately, and my staff retention rates and productivity levels have exceeded expectations at every college for which I have worked. The results speak for themselves.

One common mistake I have seen at smaller colleges is the tendency to focus on only one or two conversions, usually a lead/enrollment or a lead/application conversion. College administrators have failed to realize that many other conversions exist and matter much more to the institution's day-to-day operations. They should track these conversions on a weekly, if not daily, basis.

Tracking multiple types of conversion matters greatly because each conversion tells a different story. If you have a high conversion rate in one area and a low conversion rate in another area, the disparity exists for a reason. If you know the common reasons your metrics fall below average in one area, you can take steps to correct the problem. The repair process resembles a surgeon operating with a laser rather than with a dull axe. If you know exactly where you hurt, you can target the treatment to that specific area. You do not want to cut off your leg just because you have a scratch or cut on your thigh. Struggling colleges typically make the wrong diagnosis and tend to overtreat the illness.

This type of managing is dangerous. It will cost your college in terms of students, staff members, and revenue. You do not want your managers and staff members to crunch numbers all day, but tracking numbers matters greatly. When you know how to do this, tracking the numbers correctly takes only 30 to 40 minutes a day. It is time well spent. I once had an enrollment manager tell me that he did not want his college to focus so much on numbers because enrollment should focus on the students and not the numbers. I immediately thought, "Does he not understand that behind every one of those numbers is a student who has asked for his help?"

If you do not know the numbers for your college, you have no idea how many students are interested in your school, how many of them have received help, or how many of them are still waiting to receive assistance. The most frustrating aspect of enrollment consulting is finding enrollment managers who do not know their college's conversion rates. If the college wants to succeed, administrators should move uninformed enrollment managers to a different role or ask them to resign for gross dereliction of duty. No excuse exists for that level of incompetence, and the administration should not tolerate it. Always remember that behind each number is a real person who needs your help to attend college.

> **Always remember that behind each number is a real person who needs your help to attend college.**

The Basics

So what conversion data should an online enrollment manager track? Note the key word *online*. Online enrollment conversion expectations differ from traditional brick-and-mortar conversion expectations, and one cannot analyze the two in the same way.

Here are the seven basic types of online conversions (all are percentages):

- Lead to contact
- Contact to activity
- Activity to application
- Application to accepted
- Accepted to new start
- Lead to new start
- Application to new start

I use the term *new start* rather than *enrolled* with the last three conversion types because the term *enrolled* also frequently applies to continuing students in a non-profit college's database. If you cannot separate the two in your database, you will have useless data. With online enrollment management, you want to track new starts per term. You should track additional conversions after the students' first day of class, but, for simplicity's sake, I will cover only the seven basic conversions related to student acquisition.

Note that the term *interviewed* does not appear in the list of conversions. Most colleges track the status of pre-enrollment interviews for ground-based applicants but not necessarily for online enrollments. Many colleges will interview some online students but not all. As mentioned in a previous chapter, online students who participate in a telephone interview with an enrollment counselor start college at a higher rate than the students who do not participate in an interview. Making an interview mandatory for every online student, however, is not realistic and will cost you in terms of the number of completed applications you receive. A certain percentage of students

> Making an interview mandatory for every online student is not realistic and will cost you in terms of the number of completed applications you receive.

will always apply without contacting your enrollment department first. Ensuring that these students receive the basic information that you would give during a regular telephone interview (i.e., program information, tuition costs, fees, online expectations, admissions process, timelines, financial aid options, and the next steps they will take in the enrollment process) may be the most for which you can hope. Ideally, an enrollment counselor conveys this information to prospective students over the telephone. However, enrollment counselors may send the information by e-mail out of necessity. No matter how you choose to communicate with your students, make sure you give them all the information they will need.

Lead: Every request for information that comes with a name and one form of contact (such as a telephone number or an e-mail address)

Before reviewing each conversion type individually, we should define the term *lead*. I have heard numerous arguments regarding the definition of the term; because of this disagreement, no national standard exists for lead conversions. Here is how I define a *lead*: Every request for information that comes with a name and one form of contact (such as a telephone number or an e-mail address) constitutes a lead. Under this definition, you can use a for-profit model for your initial tracking of leads. In other words, if you have the contact information, and the student wishes to attend an online college, the request is a lead.

We should also clarify the time frame for analyzing the different types of data. Most conversions are rolling, which means that they tend to roll over from one year or month into the next. We expect this. However, you must set a starting point for when you will begin tracking your data. For conversion data (such as the number of applications or the number of accepted students), you must pick a start and end date for your data. You can use January 1 of each year, July 1 of each year, or another date as your start date. It is important that you choose a date and begin counting. For example, if you want to find your application-to-accepted conversions for applications taken during the 2009 calendar year, you should start counting on January 1, 2009 and tally every application taken during that year—no matter if the applicant enrolled, cancelled, or disappeared. You are looking for a gross number. You will then verify the number of students accepted, which will serve as your conversion percentage as of the date you pulled your accepted numbers. These numbers should improve every month after January 1, 2010 until they become flat by late spring.

> I will never forget hearing a start-up campus manager say to me, "That is not fair. Many of the applications taken at the end of the year should not count since they were applying for the fall of next year and may not get accepted until early summer . . . this will make me look bad."
>
> I wanted to say to her, "First, I never said it was going to be fair, and second, do you remember the phrase *rolling conversions*?" Some conversions will look better than they really are the first year, and some conversions will look worse.

Every campus has to start somewhere. At a start-up campus, or with a new program launch, you will have slightly skewed numbers during your first year due to rolling conversions. You must expect this. The numbers will level out in the second year, and they will prove more accurate going forward. The fact remains, you have to start somewhere.

Lead to Contact

The whole process starts with the lead-to-contact conversion. I already defined *lead*, but what is a *contact*?

> **Contact**: Either a voice-to-voice conversation between an enrollment counselor and a prospect or a direct e-mail sent from the prospect.

A contact constitutes either a voice-to-voice conversation between an enrollment counselor and a prospect or a direct e-mail sent from the prospect. Attempted or indirect contacts—such as voice mail messages or automatically generated e-mails sent to prospects—do *not* count as contacts.

As you receive leads in your computer system, you have 24-48 hours to contact the lead before you may lose your chance to do so. You have a limited amount of time because most students will have requested information from several colleges. If even one of those institutions is a for-profit college, its enrollment counselors will have probably contacted the lead within 48 hours. You should check the lead-to-contact conversion every day of the week for each counselor. A good for-profit goal is 80%, which you can only reach if you have an appropriate amount of staff members at your college. If you have inadequate staffing, find out where your numbers stand and try to improve your score. All colleges can benefit from a little improvement.

> You must work with what you have available—good or bad.

If you have a low conversion rate and it does not improve over time, do not blame the quality of your leads. Only poor musicians blame their instruments. You must work with what you have available—good or bad. If you struggle in this area and want to improve, begin looking at when your enrollment counselors attempt to contact leads and how often they do so. Do they make the mistake of calling at the same time every day? Do they call often enough? Try rotating your call schedule based on three times of the day: morning, afternoon, and evening. For example, try calling in the morning on one day and in the afternoon on the next day. If you do not successfully contact the lead at either time, call in the evening the next day and leave a voice mail message. Do not leave a message every day, because you will frustrate the lead. Leave a message only after you have attempted but failed to contact the lead three or four times.

The simplest explanation for this conversion problem is usually the most accurate as well. Unfortunately, the simplest explanation is usually a lack of persistence. Once you have a lead in your database, you may be unable to reach the lead during your first week of attempted contacts. Your enrollment counselors must persist. Prospects' lives change; you cannot know when they will feel motivated to go to school. Try again later—next week, next month, or next quarter. Persistence pays off.

Contact to Activity

Many small non-profit colleges have difficulty tracking the contact-to-activity conversion because their data management systems usually are not programmed to track enrollment statuses at this level. Still, small colleges need not despair. They can often add the missing statuses to their existing systems. That is good news, because every status tells a story.

The activity number in this conversion represents the sum of the values of all lead-status categories resulting in a positive action other than "send me some information." Information-only requests count as contacts—not as scheduled activities. Examples of activities include appointments, immediate interviews, scheduled return calls to prospects, and anything short of an application. The ultimate objective is to track how many of your leads are moving forward in the process. If your data management system tracks each status separately, simply add them together for a total activity count for your conversion

> Examples of activities include appointments, immediate interviews, scheduled return calls to prospects, and anything short of an application.

metric. The general activity number you will receive is not as direct as tracking an interview-to-application conversion but as we said earlier, some of your applicants will never have a formal telephone interview. Many times, interview information will be distributed over several different communication methods and can take place over a period of days or weeks with several email and telephone conversations mixed together. A good for-profit model for this conversion will be at least 50%. Regardless of where your contact-to-activity percentages currently stand, the key is to always keep improving.

If your percentage fails to rise, you may want to listen to the telephone conversations between your counselors and potential students. A common mistake is for counselors to ask narrow questions or make narrow statements, such as, "So, should I just wait to hear back from you?" or "Can I send you some information?" or "Call me back if you think you may be interested." New enrollment counselors often ask narrow questions when they do not know where to direct the conversation. The situation presents a perfect training opportunity.

Activity to Application

The activity-to-application conversion starts to tell the story of your success or failure. If your enrollment counselors follow up with their activities, send interview information to students, and respond quickly out of a sense of urgency, you will always have good numbers. Unfortunately, I have seen dramatically inflated numbers from many non-profit colleges because they had a seriously limited definition of a *lead*. A college administrator once told me that they were converting 90% of their leads to applications. I discovered that the college was only counting people as leads if they completed a pre-qualification interview. As you can imagine, this dramatically reduced their gross number of leads and their conversion appeared incredibly high.

A typical for-profit model for the activity-to-application conversion is a minimum of 50%. If your numbers lag, your counselors are most likely struggling with either follow-up or closing. Poor follow-up commonly results from the notion that if students are truly serious about attending college, they will take the initiative to complete the application or at least return the counselor's telephone call. Nothing reduces your application numbers more than the belief among counselors that every prospect knows what to do, how to do it, and when to do it. These are risky assumptions. Always remember, many prospective students will start to complete your college's application online but never submit it and never contact you again. Consistent follow-up is the key to this conversion.

> A typical for-profit model for the activity-to-application conversion is a minimum of 50%.

Application to Accepted

Never guess when it comes to the application-to-accepted conversion. You already know how to calculate the percentages for your ground-based programs, and you probably report them every year to the Department of Education. If you are just starting to offer programs online and have no reference for these conversions, use your ground conversion numbers as a baseline for your online programs the first year.

A typical for-profit application-to-accepted conversion is a minimum of 50-60%. Even though some non-profit colleges may boast a similar conversion rate, the real difference comes in the amount of applications taken and

> A typical for-profit application-to-accepted conversion is a minimum of 50-60%.

the level of follow up and support given by your enrollment staff. Some colleges believe that having a low acceptance rate is a "badge of honor" and demonstrates how selective their institution has become. Being highly selective in your traditional ground-based programs may be exactly what your college desires, but you must remember why your institution decided to launch online programs in the first place (increase revenue). You cannot grow your online program with a 25% online acceptance rate. That being said, even if your accepted rate exceeds 50%, you cannot grow your program if the initial number of applications is below what is needed to hit your goal. Remember, one conversion leads to the next and all tell a different story. You may have a perfectly respectable 55% conversion rate in this area, but if the conversions leading up to this one are dramatically low, your net enrollments will suffer.

> Many college administrators believe they excel at their work if they have at least one high conversion rate, even if their other conversion rates are low.

Many college administrators believe they excel at their work if they have at least one high conversion rate, even if their other conversion rates are low. They mistakenly believe that if they miss their enrollment goals, it is because they have too few leads or insufficient interest in the college's online programs. Nothing could be further from the truth.

Accepted to New Start

Most colleges also report their accepted-to-new start conversion—often referred to as accepted-to-enrolled conversion—every year. When I asked a vice president of enrollment to tell me how many new enrollments his school had last year, he reported an unusually high number. He said he counted not only *new* students but also *returning* students. He reasoned that since the returning students were also enrolling in classes, they too should be counted. I told him that I was referring to *new* enrollments or *new starts* only, and asked him if he could provide me with that data. He had no answer to that question because of the way new enrollments are coded in his college's computer system. I was somewhat shocked that he could not find the data, but later realized that this issue is fairly common in smaller schools with older computer systems. Regardless of the system that is being used, if an enrollment department bases its success on enrollment growth, then administrators need to track both categories of enrollment: new and old.

> If an enrollment department bases its success on enrollment growth, then administrators need to track both categories of enrollment: new and old.

When it comes to the accepted-to-new start conversion, a typical for-profit college may be 79% or higher. At a typical four-year, nonprofit college, the percentage is closer to 31% (U.S. Department of Education, 2007). Although many non-profit colleges will argue that their percentage is low due to the volume of applications, this argument does not explain the low new start rates. The argument may be valid if they are trying to explain why an application-to-accepted percentage is low, but not why after all of the hoops and hurdles have been addressed, and students have been accepted to the institution, do such a large percentage of accepted students never actually start classes.

Why do so many for-profit colleges emphasize this number and use it to gauge the overall effectiveness of their enrollment process and enrollment growth? It is because this conversion is a direct reflection of the enrollment process itself. A well thought out, student-friendly acceptance process with consistent follow-up will typically result in higher start rates. Most students know a college's qualifications

> A well thought out, student-friendly acceptance process with consistent follow-up will typically result in higher start rates.

when they apply for admission. The success or failure of an enrollment plan directly relates to a college's ability to process the application, accept the student, and begin classes quickly. High conversions in every area but this one will mean nothing if students do not start classes. If your college is struggling in this area, you are not alone. For many non-profit colleges, the acceptance process can be a long, drawn-out and frustrating experience. The solutions, on paper at least, are usually easy to develop. However, non-profit colleges may have difficulty implementing the solution in a bureaucratic environment.

Before drafting a plan of action, consider these questions: Does your college still use paper application forms or require letters of recommendation on paper rather than in an electronic format? Do your online students have a voice-to-voice interview with a financial aid representative? How many start dates does your college offer to new students? Is there a process for follow-up after the student is accepted?

> Does your college still use paper application forms or require letters of recommendation on paper rather than in an electronic format? Do your online students have a voice-to-voice interview with a financial aid representative? How many start dates does your college offer to new students? Is there a process for follow-up after the student is accepted?

Although many of these items can be corrected easily, many others will require correction at the highest level of the institution since dragging a college into the 21st century can be very difficult. It is amazing how many colleges have fallen behind when it comes to electronic document processing and still require paper. Online students choose to go online for convenience. If the application and acceptance process is not quick and convenient, they will go elsewhere.

> Online students choose to go online for convenience. If the application and acceptance process is not quick and convenient, they will go elsewhere.

Lead to New Start

Enrollment managers quote the conversion of leads to new starts more than any other conversion discussed in this chapter, even though it has only marginal significance. The marginalization of this conversion stems from the lack of an industry-standard definition of *lead*. If you define *lead* as requests for information that come with a name and a form of contact, then the lead-to-new start conversion can provide a wealth of information. If you narrow your definition of lead or tailor it uniquely for your college, your calculated conversion percentage has value only to you and only if you consistently apply the same standard each year.

Consider this example: Your director of enrollment retired last year. Before leaving, she counted every lead with a name and a contact option and calculated a conversion rate of 3%. Your new director of enrollment counted as leads only those students who requested information about a specific program offered at your college and were successfully contacted via telephone. Your new director then calculated a conversion rate of 12%. Have your statistics improved? You cannot know for sure. Struggling enrollment managers treasure this type of conversion. As long as they are allowed to define a lead, they can make their department look good while shifting the blame to others.

> Unless you have a consistent and ironclad definition for *lead*, your lead-to-new start conversion percentage will never mean anything more than what your enrollment manager wants it to mean.

Unless you have a consistent and ironclad definition for *lead*, your lead-to-new start conversion percentage will never mean anything more than what your enrollment manager wants it to mean. You cannot compare it with a competitor's number or find a national average, because no such average exists. Only sales representatives from pay-per-lead providers who want you to buy their service will tell you that a national average exists for the lead-to-new start conversion. A national average does not exist, because *lead* has no nationally accepted definition. Until consensus is reached, confine your comparisons to yearly numbers at your own college if you want to derive value from the lead-to-new start conversion.

Application to New Start

I love the application-to-new start conversion because it helps me develop forecasts. It blends process with performance and gives me a sense of where my gross new start numbers are headed based on my current application totals. For example, if I know that my team will convert 50% of the applications we receive to new starts, I will have a reasonable estimate of my new start totals even if some of my applications have not cleared the acceptance process. The application-to-new start conversion also helps me pace the flow of applications so that they do not all arrive just before the start of classes. For example, I need 100 new starts for a cohort starting classes in 10 weeks, and the application deadline is 9 weeks away. Assume I have 110 applications now, and they are converting at a rate of 50%. That means I need 90 more applications over the next 9 weeks to reach my goal. Since my enrollment staff works 5 days a week, I will set my staff's goal at 10 applications a week or an average of two applications a day. Remember, each college has a different conversion rate, but the average for-profit college converts around 40-50% of its gross applications. If your percentage falls short, consider looking at your application and follow-up process.

> The application-to-new start conversion also helps me pace the flow of applications so that they do not all arrive just before the start of classes.

> Remember, each college has a different conversion rate, but the average for-profit college converts around 40-50% of its gross applications.

Many for-profit colleges will apply what is known as the 30-40-30 rule, which states that 30% of applicants will start college regardless of what you do or the quality of your staff and 30% probably will not start college regardless of what you do or the quality of your staff. So, focus on the 40% in the middle. If you can convert half of them (20%), you will convert a combined

50% of your applicants into starts. If you convert at a rate of 30% or less, you have a problem. Look at the activity-to-application and application-to-accepted conversions for the answer.

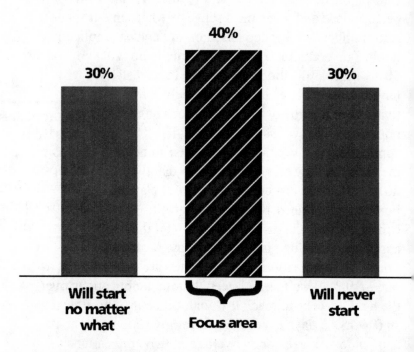

Chapter Summary

This chapter discussed the importance of interpreting and using conversion data for managing operations and tracking enrollment management success. The chapter provided guidelines for using conversion data and then discussed seven conversions especially suited to enrollment management: lead to contact, contact to activity, activity to application, application to accepted, accepted to new start, lead to new start, and application to new start.

Chapter Seven

Advertising Costs per Status

(Cost per Lead, Application, and Enrollment)

This chapter covers the following **key points**:

- » Marketing expenditures
- » Tracking lead type and lead source
- » Analyzing cost per lead
- » Analyzing cost per application
- » Analyzing cost per enrollment

If you want to shock the staff members at your college, tell them how much your school spends each year on marketing. If you want to terrify an enrollment department, tell them they are responsible for every dollar your school spends on marketing. Leads—even bad ones— cost money.

> Leads—even bad ones—cost money.

As an enrollment manager or enrollment counselor, you own the leads. What will you do with them? An enrollment counselor complained to me one time that it was not her fault that only a few of the leads assigned to her ever enrolled. She said that half of her leads were "bad," and it was not her fault that she did not have quality leads. She was surprised when I responded, "Half? If only half of your leads are bad, then you are the luckiest enrollment counselor in the world!"

Unfortunately, she is not alone. Many enrollment counselors, enrollment managers, and senior administrators fall into the same trap. They share the mistaken impression that the job of enrolling students should take little work, believing that all "good" leads want to attend college or they would not have requested information. To carry the thought process further, if leads do not call after receiving an automatically generated e-mail thanking them for requesting information, it probably means that these people are bad leads and the enrollment counselor should discard them. Now, imagine that each request for information, good or bad, costs your college an average of $50. If your college converts 3% of its leads every year, well…it's enough to give a person heartburn.

How many people at your college would you trust with $500,000 or more every year? Now

> How many people at your college would you trust with $500,000 or more every year?

look at the enrollment counselors at your college. You are giving them the money every time you assign them a new lead. To get a good return on your investment, it is vital to track every lead and make sure that your school is putting every advertising dollar to good use.

Cost per Lead

Are some leads better than others? Sure they are. Do some leads convert better than others? Sure they do. If you do not know what works at your college and what doesn't, it is fairly simple to create the process from scratch. You can track this information by analyzing conversion rates by lead type and lead source in a spreadsheet. First, you need to prepare your data. Divide your leads according to their type and source, and create a separate tab in your spreadsheet for each group. A lead type is a general term used to describe a broad category. Some examples of lead types include media, referral, non-media, and recycled.

For each lead type, group the leads according to the source of the lead. Let us use media leads as an example. Media leads include Web-based sources such as banner ads and pay-per-click campaigns, direct mailings, radio spots, and newspaper advertisements. Build a separate column for each source. Do the same for the other three lead types; referral, non-media, and recycled. Sources for referrals include students, faculty members, alumni, enrollment counselors, and other staff members. These leads cost no money, and who doesn't love a free lead? Non-media leads flow from non-media events and presentations, such as an open house, a college fair, or a high school presentation. These leads typically carry a price tag, depending on the source and the investment needed for staging the event or presentation.

Lead Type

Type	Total Leads	Costs	Locked CPL	Locked % of Total	Locked % of Costs
Media	1888	$100,000	$53	28%	67%
Non-Media	3877	$50,000	$13	58%	33%
Referral	462		$0	7%	0%
Recycled	487		$0	7%	0%
Totals	6714	$150,000	$22	100%	100%

Lead Source

Media

Source	Total Leads	Costs	Locked CPL	Locked % of Source Total	Locked % of Costs
TV	268	$20,000	$75	14%	20%
Web site	467	$5,000	$11	25%	5%
Radio	36	$10,000	$278	2%	10%
Newspaper	15	$1,200	$80	1%	1%
Magazine	24	$4,000	$167	1%	4%
Billboard	69	$5,000	$72	4%	5%
Direct Mail	759	$48,300	$64	40%	48%
Pay-Per-Click	150	$1,500	$10	8%	2%
Pay-Per-Lead	100	$5,000	$50	5%	5%
TOTALS	1888	$100,000	$53	100%	100%

Non Media

Source	Total Leads	Costs	Locked CPL	Locked % of Source Total	Locked % of Costs
College Fairs	2269	$30,000	$13	59%	60%
HS Events	1608	$20,000	$12	41%	40%
TOTALS	3877	$50,000	$13	100%	100%

Referral

Source	Total Leads	Costs	Locked CPL	Locked % of Source Total	Locked % of Costs
Student	326	$0	$0	71%	0%
Staff	89	$0	$0	19%	0%
Alumni	47	$0	$0	10%	0%
TOTALS	462	$0	$0	100%	0%

Recycled

Source	Total Leads	Costs	Locked CPL	Locked % of Source Total	Locked % of Costs
College Board	24	$0	$0	5%	0%
Web site	158	$0	$0	32%	0%
Radio	1	$0	$0	0%	0%
Newspaper	0	$0	$0	0%	0%
Magazine	0	$0	$0	0%	0%
Billboard	0	$0	$0	0%	0%
Direct Mail	138	$0	$0	28%	0%
Pay-Per-Click	2	$0	$0	0%	0%
Pay-Per-Lead	3	$0	$0	1%	0%
College Fair	28	$0	$0	6%	0%
HS Event	67	$0	$0	14%	0%
Student Ref	38	$0	$0	8%	0%
Staff Ref	19	$0	$0	4%	0%
Alumni Ref	9	$0	$0	2%	0%
TOTALS	487	$0	$0	100%	0%

The next best thing to a referral is a recycled lead, because the latter also costs no money. A recycled lead can be a media lead that originally came from a previous fiscal year's advertising budget and has been resurrected in the current year. Here is an example of a recycled lead: John contacted you after seeing a print advertisement for your college last year, but was unable to attend your college due to a conflict with his work schedule. He inquired again yesterday and now wants to apply. Note, however, that while the lead *type* changed (from media to recycled), the *source* remains the same. In your spreadsheet, make sure you code the lead as a *recycled* lead and not as a current-year *media* lead. The *original* lead came from an older marketing piece and not from the print advertisements you have paid for and run this year. When you attribute the lead to the correct type and source, you can learn which advertising pieces are working and which ones are not. If you incorrectly attribute a recycled lead to the current year's advertising, you may think that the current advertisement is producing more results than it really is. You do not want to make the mistake of reinvesting in an advertising piece that did not produce.

> A recycled lead can be a media lead that originally came from a previous fiscal year's advertising budget and has been resurrected in the current year.

> If you incorrectly attribute a recycled lead to the current year's advertising, you may think that the current advertisement is producing more results than it really is.

The next step in preparing your data is to find the lead type and source for each new student who requested information during the last fiscal year—this means every lead in your database that you received during the prior fiscal year. It does not matter if the lead cancelled or enrolled. You want gross numbers. If you have not been tracking leads by advertising type and source and have to sort through your database to find the information, the process could take a long time, but it is well worth the effort.

Let's say you found the following information from your research: You received 9,000 total leads during the last fiscal year for your online programs; 6,000 came from media sources, 2,000 came from non-media events and presentations, 600 came from referrals, and 400 were recycled. For each of these leads, you had the forethought to code them according to the specific type and source when you originally entered them into your database.

	A	B
1	**Media**	6,000
2	**Non-Media**	2,000
3	**Referrals**	600
4	**Recycled**	400
5	**Total**	9,000 Leads

Now look at every dime you spent on advertising during the last fiscal year, separating media expenses from non-media expenses. Let's say that you spent $400,000 total. You spent $350,000 on media purchases and $50,000 on non-media events. Remember, your referrals and recycled leads cost nothing. Your overall cost per lead (CPL) is $400,000/9,000 leads, but your specific CPL by lead type is $350,000/6,000 and $50,000/2,000. Next, calculate exactly what you spent per lead source (e.g., print media, pay-per-click, etc.) Apply the same formula: Divide the dollar amount by the total number of leads generated for that lead source.

Recycled leads and referrals are slightly different and can have a long shelf-life. Even though the lead counts as a recycled lead *type*, the lead counts under the specific lead *source*. Therefore, every time you recycle an old media lead, you recoup your costs from the prior fiscal year, and your average cost for that source *this* year goes down. In other words, the shelf-life of a media lead never expires; every time you convert a media lead to a recycled lead, you get part of your money back.

> Every time you convert a media lead to a recycled lead, you get part of your money back.

Cost per Application

As you did with your leads, you must now group your applications according to type and source. Your enrollment budgeting projections will rely greatly on computing your cost per application. First, you must find the data for every application that came in during the last fiscal year. To help with your data search, remember the principles behind rolling conversions: It does not matter in which fiscal year you created the original lead since many of your applications will come from referrals and recycled leads. Your goal is to compute an average cost per application according to type and media source.

> Your goal is to compute an average cost per application according to type and media source.

Let's say that 1,800 applications came in during the last fiscal year. Now group the applications according to lead type and source, and use the same dollar amounts (i.e., $350,000 and $50,000, respectively) as you did when you calculated the CPL. Let's further assume that from the 1,800 applications you received, 900 came from media sources, 500 came from non-media sources, 200 came from referrals, and 200 came from recycled leads. If you use the same dollar amounts per type (i.e., $350,000 and $50,000, respectively) that you used for the CPL, you can calculate precisely your overall cost per application (CPA) for the last fiscal year. Next, calculate exactly what you spent per lead source (e.g., print media, pay-per-click, etc.). Apply the same formula:

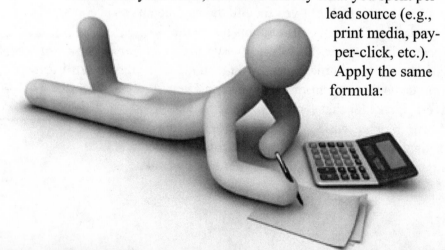

Divide the dollar amount by the total number of leads generated for that lead source. You will likely find that many of the types and sources that generate the most *leads* do not generate the most *applications*. Different leads convert at different levels, which is ultimately what you are trying to analyze along with your costs.

> Many of the types and sources that generate the most *leads* do not generate the most *applications*.

Cost per Enrollment

Cost per enrollment is the final spending category that you must analyze. As you did with leads and applications, you need to find the data for every new enrollment from the last fiscal year. You are only looking for new students who have never taken a class at your college. Again, remember the concept of rolling conversions, and do not worry if many of your enrollments came from leads and even applications generated during a previous fiscal year.

The ultimate goal is to create a statistical model to use when you prepare your new enrollment budget and decide where to spend your advertising dollars. Use the same type and source calculation formulas and procedures for enrollments as you used for leads and applications. You will find that many of the lead types and sources that generated the most applications may not have generated the most enrollments.

> The ultimate goal is to create a statistical model to use when you prepare your new enrollment budget and decide where to spend your advertising dollars.

It sounds like a lot of work, but do not feel discouraged; use the situation as a training opportunity. If you find that a particular lead source is generating applications but not enrollments, you should ask yourself these questions: What is unique about that specific lead source? Who are they? Do applications generated from those particular lead sources require more or less attention? When are applications falling out of the process?

You are looking for patterns in the data. You may discover, for example, that leads that converted to applications and originated from a Web site lead source converted poorly to enrollments. Why did that happen? Was the gap between the lead creation date and the application date extremely small? Did the leads apply the same day that they requested information? A good enrollment manager will find all of this data valuable. From this information, you can determine the leads that convert best to applications and then to enrollments. Once you have discovered these specific high-converting leads, ensure that your enrollment counselors make them a priority.

> From this information, you can determine the leads that convert best to applications and then to enrollments.

You also may find that some of the leads that convert the best are referral and recycled leads. Referrals usually have a champion they trust. If a friend or relative made the referral, the friend or relative becomes your greatest ally in the enrollment process. Referrals generated from existing students prove even better than those from other sources. Current or former online students have already jumped through all the hoops, they know the good and the bad and the pros and the cons about your online programs, and they were sufficiently impressed to convince a friend or relative to enroll.

Recycled leads, on the other hand, have already expressed an interest in your school and are now coming back to you. Many times, recycled leads have already participated in an interview and know a lot about your online programs. Even better, they may have tried another college in the interim and, after discovering that the other college did not meet their expectations, they came to the realization that your college provided a better fit for them. These leads have an extremely high conversion rate. To make sure that you do not lose them again, you must work with them the minute you receive an inquiry. Many of these recycled leads may have left another college because they believed that the school viewed them as nothing more than a number. Now is your chance to show these returning leads that your college does care about their educational future. Show them that your college is different, and all of your enrollment management planning will pay off.

Chapter Summary

This chapter emphasized the relationship between marketing expenditures for advertising and enrollment management. In particular, the chapter explained how to distinguish lead types from lead sources and how to use those determinations in analyzing cost per lead, cost per application, and cost per enrollment. It provided step-by-step directions for completing the analyses, and it offered explanations for using your results to more efficiently manage the enrollment division at your college, prepare your enrollment budget, and allocate marketing dollars for optimum cost-effectiveness and to generate the best results.

Chapter Eight

Managing the Enrollment Team

This chapter covers the following **key points**:

> » Common challenges for enrollment managers and directors of enrollment
>
> » Balancing responsibility and reward for enrollment counselors
>
> » Establishing accountability and tracking goals
>
> » Managing strengths and weaknesses of an enrollment team
>
> » Using performance reviews and performance-improvement plans with an enrollment team
>
> » Setting the bar for work ethic
>
> » Managing employee attitudes
>
> » Defining *dedication*
>
> » Importance of team skills for enrollment management

When it comes to enrollment, many for-profit colleges have a serious problem with staff turnover, which results in part from the constant pressure that for-profit directors of enrollment feel to produce results. A much more serious underlying cause of the problem involves the average for-profit enrollment manager's inexperience.

When I began working at the University of Phoenix, I had served as a director of enrollment for several years at other for-profit colleges, so I was no rookie. As time passed and I met other enrollment directors from across the country, I learned that nearly all of these directors had worked in the industry for just a couple of years and most of them had been in their positions for less than 6 months.

Granted, the University of Phoenix was notorious for churning and burning its enrollment counselors, but the number of directors who also cycled out after less than a year in the position shocked me. Seasoned professionals have enough difficulty performing well as enrollment directors, but rookies with less than 3 years in the industry must have an even harder time. Most of the directors I met had started as enrollment counselors and probably had produced top results. After a year or so, they were promoted to enrollment managers. Their colleges were growing so fast and desperately needed new directors. After a year or so as successful enrollment managers, they were promoted to campus directors of enrollment.

As a student of history, I found the leadership crisis within the University of Phoenix akin to the U.S. Army during wartime mobilization. Young college graduates with little or no experience were being commissioned as lieutenants and given a platoon of soldiers to lead into combat. These new officers were often killed in their first few months at war, but the ones who survived were quickly moved up the chain of command to fill the increasing leadership needs of an ever-expanding army.

Management may be a science, but leadership is definitely an art. The difference between the two is massive, especially when dealing with the types of personalities you need to build a solid enrollment team. Some enrollment teams at the University of Phoenix had a 100% turnover each year—including enrollment managers and the directors of enrollment. My campus, however, consistently posted one of the lowest turnover rates in the university system while setting records for production and profitability. I do not mean this as a criticism of the culture or the atmosphere at the University of Phoenix; I loved the fast pace and the results-oriented culture. I left the University of Phoenix because the college had simply grown too big and too fast as a result of its highly efficient business model. When you grow too fast, you will become desperate to fill positions, which can often lead to bad hires.

> **The qualities I look for in an enrollment counselor typically reside in people who have a passion for education and for helping people.**

Some of the qualities I look for in an enrollment counselor—friendliness, outgoing personality, and high energy—typically reside in people who have a passion for education and for helping people. Such people, however, can take a lot of effort to manage.

Responsibility and Reward

Let us assume that you are an enrollment manager with five enrollment counselors working for you. Let us also assume that you followed the tips presented in this book and selected individuals with the qualities and personality traits appropriate for the job. They passed your telephone interview, completed the training program, officially joined the team, and have been working for at least 3 months.

Now what? How do you keep them motivated to produce results every day? How do you keep them focused on their conversions, their call volume, their goals, and the reality that every number has a human being behind it, and they have a personal and professional responsibility to help every lead, applicant, and enrolled student assigned to them?

First, you must ensure that every enrollment counselor (indeed, every employee at the college) understands the value of the enrollment counselor position. Some people work well under pressure, while others melt like a snowball in July. Over the years, I have learned that people can handle all the pressure you give them if they honestly and deeply believe that the stress comes with the pursuit of a great and noble cause; no cause is nobler than changing a life through education.

> First, you must ensure that every enrollment counselor (indeed, every employee at the college) understands the value of the enrollment counselor position.

First, enrollment counselors and enrollment managers need to understand that every dollar spent, every raise given, and every paycheck issued rests in their hands. In enrollment management, if we fail, people lose their jobs. If we do not reach our goals, instructors and staff members face termination, and salaries do not increase. If the school lays off a staff member because too few students have enrolled in the program, the fault lies with us. We failed. We failed to call enough old leads. We failed to find the students who truly want to pursue higher education but have been buried in our database. We failed to service many of the students who applied to the college but then withdrew their applications. We failed to convince enough prospects that our college is different and that we really do care about our students.

> In enrollment management, if we fail, people lose their jobs. If the school lays off a staff member because too few students have enrolled in the program, the fault lies with us. We failed.

117

This may sound harsh, but I tell this to all applicants for the position of enrollment counselor before I hire them. I explain to them the heavy responsibility of the position but remind them that it comes with a great reward. Perhaps I sound overly sentimental, but a good enrollment counselor will change a life. If an enrollment counselor takes the time to work with a nervous adult student who has been out of school for 10 years and helps to build the student's self-confidence and self-esteem, then I assure you that the enrollment counselor's efforts will yield life-changing results for the student. A good enrollment counselor will change not only the student's destiny but also the student's family for generations to come.

> A good enrollment counselor will change not only the student's destiny but also the student's family for generations to come.

You will never have a team willing to go the extra mile when the members have nothing to motivate them to even try. Phrases such as "meeting the enrollment goal," "getting a new cohort off the ground," or "hitting revenue" do not motivate a team to give more than 100%. On the other hand, highly motivated, caring individuals focused on a noble mission will work extremely hard to meet their goals. These individuals will call every lead the same day they receive them, pursue every application, and share ownership in the success of the students they have been assigned to help. You want these individuals to work on your team.

> Highly motivated, caring individuals focused on a noble mission will work extremely hard to meet their goals.

Accountability and Goals

Now that a noble mission motivates your staff, you need to manage the responsibility side of the equation. As an enrollment manager, my staff members always knew that I took education quite seriously. One can easily lose focus trying to help every student at the level I demand. The enrollment manager has a responsibility to keep everyone on track, focused, and accountable for his or her daily activities.

The phrase A + B = C has never been more true than when applied to online enrollment management. Unfortunately, no magic conversion exists that will make your enrollment troubles vanish. However, I have seen a specific cause-and-effect relationship in the world of college enrollment. If you know where you have been and where you are now, you can reasonably predict your final destination. Phone calls generate contacts. Contacts generate activities. Activities generate applications. Applications produce accepted students, and accepted students result in new enrollments. It isn't rocket science.

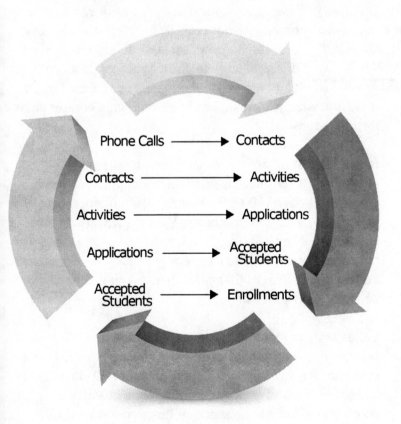

Phone Calls ⟶ Contacts

Contacts ⟶ Activities

Activities ⟶ Applications

Applications ⟶ Accepted Students

Accepted Students ⟶ Enrollments

That being said, you first need to know where you have been. Every conversion speaks volumes, and you need to know how to interpret what the conversion tells you. If you know, based on your team's past performance, that it takes 100 applications to produce 50 accepted students, and you also know that 50 accepted students generally translates into 25 new enrollments, then you just need to figure out your start goal, how much time you have to reach your goal, and how much activity it takes for your team to produce 100 applications.

Let us assume that you have five enrollment counselors and your college has four terms starting per year. Your team can efficiently handle a finite number of new applications, so you need to determine how many an average counselor can handle based on your college's performance history, process, and support staff. Every college is different, and no golden rule exists when it comes to production goals per counselor. You must find what *your* team has been averaging and set goals for improvement.

> Every college is different, and no golden rule exists when it comes to production goals per counselor.

If you have a five-member team, your team has been averaging 100 enrollments per counselor, and you have a goal this year of 600 enrollments, you will not meet your goal unless you immediately hire at least two more counselors. New counselors will produce in their first year only about half of what an experienced counselor produces. To reach your goal of 600 enrollments, you will need five veterans and two rookies.

Let us assume that it is January 15 and you met your January new-enrollment goal. Now you are planning your midterm start in March. You have a goal of 60 enrollments and assign each of your five counselors a goal of 12 enrollments. Let's look at one of those counselors, Jill.

Jill is an experienced counselor who has been working for you for more than a year. Your next term starts on March 24, and Jill has a goal of 12 new enrollments for that term. She already has 20 gross applications, and five of them have been accepted. You know that she has an application/ accepted conversion rate of 50% and an accepted/new start conversion rate of 40%. To reach her goal, she needs at least 60 total applications, which translates into 30 accepted applications. Those 30 accepted applications probably will give her a net of 12 new students in March.

Unfortunately, the application deadline is only 8 weeks away, and Jill has a lot of work left to reach her goal. She still needs at least 40 more applications. She knows that she will need to average at least five applications each week until the application deadline. She works an average of 5 days a week, so she must produce an average of one application for every day she works. Since you have been tracking her conversions, you know that Jill usually converts 50% of her solid activities and interviews into applications. You deduce that she must conduct at least two telephone interviews per day to average one application per day. You also have been watching her call levels and know that Jill usually needs to spend an average of an hour and a half on calls to her new leads, old leads, and recycled leads to schedule one solid telephone interview. You also know that Jill usually takes 1 hour to complete a solid telephone interview. In addition, you must factor in the follow-up calls she makes to her existing applicants and scheduled return calls to her accepted students. You calculate that she will spend an average of at least 2 hours a day on these follow-up calls.

How many hours each day, from now until the March deadline, must Jill spend on the telephone? The answer is 7 hours a day. Nobody said it was an easy job, and I hope you have a new appreciation for what successful enrollment counselors endure every day. Since they spend so many hours daily on the telephone, enrollment counselors must enjoy their jobs. Granted, this is an extreme example, but it details exactly what a manager needs to know. Managers must be able to explain to counselors exactly what they need to do every day to reach their goals and pay the bills. Does this create a lot of pressure? Yes, it does; however, the school needs to cut paychecks and pay the bills. The people who write the checks are relying on us—members of the enrollment department—to bring in the cash for the college.

> Managers must be able to explain to counselors exactly what they need to do every day to reach their goals and pay the bills.

As a manager, you need to know these numbers for your team as a whole and for each of your enrollment counselors. If Jill fell too far behind to meet her goal, you would know in time to take action to make up for the difference. I never want to hear from an enrollment manager after the team has missed a goal that he or she never saw it coming. A good manager should know weeks and even months in advance exactly where the numbers are headed and whether the team has a solid chance of reaching its goals. If the numbers point toward meeting the team's goal, but the team ends up missing its goal, I will respect that and understand completely. This type of situation will happen occasionally because managers' expectations represent averages—not precise data points. On the other hand, if the numbers showed that the team would fall far short of its goals, and the managers never saw it coming, the school needs better enrollment management to succeed.

Strengths and Weaknesses

Managers really must know their enrollment numbers, because every counselor is different and will convert at different levels based on individual strengths and weaknesses. Remember, these numbers are averages; rarely will you find one counselor who meets or exceeds each average. Some of my best enrollment counselors had poor results on at least one conversion. We can expect that to happen. The more you try to correct the weakness, the more you may end up hurting the person's strengths. Not every weakness needs correction, especially if a specific strength compensates for the deficiency.

Assume Jill has an abysmal time motivating herself in the morning so that by noon, she consistently has made the fewest calls in the office. Her manager does not reprimand her for it. On the contrary, Jill performs well as an enrollment counselor, and her manager knows her strengths and weaknesses. She may not be a "calling machine" in the morning, but when she does speak to someone on the telephone, she interviews better than anyone else on her team. Her manager knows that Jill does not need to make as many calls as some of the other team members because Jill has a much higher conversion rate from activity to application. Jill knows how much telephone time she needs every day because her manager shows her the numbers and helps her understand them.

Jill's strength is her ability to bond with prospects. She is friendly, upbeat, and personable. She listens to her students and can identify their specific needs. She knows her manager trusts her telephone interviewing skills and bases that trust on her consistent conversions in this area. In return, Jill appreciates her boss and work environment, and she finds satisfaction in her work.

An inexperienced manager might believe that if Jill increased her call volume in the morning, she would produce even more. An inexperienced manager would not take the time to understand why Jill does not produce as much in the morning and may not even care. An inexperienced manager would force Jill to keep up with the rest of the team and match their morning call volume.

In contrast, an experienced manager will take Jill's life situation into consideration. Jill has two children, and her husband works second shift at his job. Jill often stays up late waiting for her husband to come home so she can see him for a few minutes a day. Jill's manager knows that although everyone has a personal life outside of work and that one should not interfere with the other, personal life can affect work life. Your staff members will always have a life outside of work, and sometimes the two overlap. The trick lies in understanding which aspects of the job might be affected and then devising ways to compensate for the overlap.

A long story short: Jill stays up late every night to see her husband. She does not feel perky at 9 a.m. because of the hours she keeps at home. She knows that feeling sluggish in the morning will cost her precious telephone calling time. Jill knows she needs to make the most of every call in the afternoon to compensate for her morning call-volume deficiency. She has the people skills to make it work. She achieves great success despite being a morning slug. Let her be a slug.

Reviews

One of the most common misconceptions in higher education is the belief that you cannot relate enrollment performance to an evaluation. Although you cannot directly base an enrollment counselor's evaluation on production, the numbers speak for themselves. Usually, poor performance is based on poor attitude and/or poor work ethic, and every evaluation should include these items. It is not "all about the numbers," but the numbers come from hard work, and each college has its own culture and level of performance-based standards.

I loved that in the for-profit world, you earned your reward if you did well; if you failed, you did not earn the reward. Those of us who worked hard, studied our positions, and took our positions to new levels received our reward. Those who did not do so suffered the consequences. This approach works well.

Next, I will discuss what workplace professionals commonly refer to as *soft skills*. Soft skills are all of the non-quantitative skills that play just as vital of a role in helping your department achieve success as the hard numbers.

> **Soft Skills**: All of the non-quantitative skills that play just as vital of a role in helping your department achieve success as the hard numbers.

The soft skills that you should consider during an evaluation include work ethic, attitude, dedication, and team skills. If a counselor excels in these areas, the enrollment numbers will come in time with good training and good day-to-day management. On the other hand, if a counselor has all of these attributes and fails, I would scrutinize the enrollment manager. Managers also need to develop expertise in these soft skills.

Work Ethic

How you define the term *work ethic* depends on the bar your manager sets. If your manager does not set the example for the team, you need to replace your manager.

What is a good work ethic? Does it mean that all of your staff members should arrive at work early and leave late and never complain or ask for compensation? Does it mean they need to be productive 100% of the time, all day, 5 days a week, all year long? Of course not. If you have a good work ethic, you know that you have an obligation to your employer to do what is necessary in a timely manner. You know that you should arrive on time, make yourself available when you are needed, and eagerly complete your work during every scheduled shift.

Work Ethic: You know that you should arrive on time, make yourself available when you are needed, and eagerly complete your work during every scheduled shift.

When I worked as a regional manager for a retail chain, an employee appealed her evaluation to me because her manager gave her a low score under the work-ethic category. I invited her manager into my office and asked him why she received such a low score. He told me that she was the only employee who did not stay late and that she left every evening at 6 p.m. sharp (which was the time her shift ended). I asked him if she was getting her work done before 6 p.m. I also asked if he had ever asked her to stay late or come in early to complete an additional assignment and if she ever refused to do so. He said, "No. She gets her work done, but she is the only one out the door every night at 6 p.m. Everyone else stays at least a few minutes past their time . . . she sets a bad example for the rest of the team."

I almost wrote him up on the spot. I have worked as a manager for a long time, and I have done more evaluations than I can remember. I have never heard anything so ridiculous. She gets all of her work done on time, has never refused additional work, and she receives a low score in work ethic because she works efficiently. It makes no sense. Many managers are Type A personalities and may put in long hours and dedicate much more of their time to their job than necessary. This does not set a good example. It sets an unrealistic example. Enrollment counselors have a highly stressful position. From the minute they walk through the door in the morning, they face work demands on several fronts. They must make telephone calls, interview prospects, and assist students in completing applications. Enrollment counselors and enrollment managers will never complete every task by the end of the day. If you did not scribble at least 20 tasks on your to-do list for tomorrow, you probably did not have time to write them all down. Remember, your staff members have a life outside of work. As long as they take care of their responsibilities, you must keep the work-ethic expectations reasonable. Not everyone has the drive of a Type A personality, and that is good. Otherwise, you would not find balance in the workplace.

Attitude

With attitude, you should always have high expectations. Employees with bad attitudes are difficult to manage and their offending behaviors are perhaps impossible to correct. If you had the misfortune of not detecting the bad attitude during the hiring interview and must now deal with the situation, good luck. Most likely, every person reading this book has struggled working with, working for, or working over someone who was infested to the core with a bad attitude. We all know the characteristics, and I will mention only a few of them here.

 **Whiners**

Whiners can find pain and anguish in a photograph of puppies and baby bunnies sleeping together. They complain about everything, and nothing you do will satisfy them. The office is too cold. The office is too hot. Their desk is too small. The computers are too slow. Their leads are all bad. Their students don't listen. Their telephone rings too loud. Their office is too noisy. Their appointments all cancel. Their hair hurts.

What do you do with people like this? You have limited options available. As a manager, you can only try to prevent these people from bringing down the rest of the team. Every office has a whiner. If you can insulate the rest of your team from the whiner, the whiner cannot harm the team and may even produce decent results.

 Pointers

No matter what happens—whether it is trivial or serious—these people will point it out every time. They miss nothing and tend to look for inconsistencies in policies or events. These people will spend 2 hours reading the staff handbook to find a regulation a coworker has broken. They have too much misdirected energy but can develop into good enrollment counselors. You need to get them on the telephone early in the day. Perhaps give them an enormous list of old leads (maybe 500 or so). The sooner you give them a time-consuming task, the better off everyone will be.

 Ph.D.s in All Things Education-Related

You find these people working in enrollment departments across the country. They are deadly to your team if you do not put them in their place. They work in the enrollment field only because they have no place else to go in your college and will quit their job the minute they complete their degree or find a job at a larger, more prestigious college. They do not respect your institution and feel the need to criticize your college at every turn. You might justify criticizing a college for poor student service; however, you cannot justify criticizing your institution's educational values and core beliefs. If any of these people work in your online division, beware. Move them out the door as soon as possible.

 Correctors

Everyone makes mistakes—including managers. There is a time and a place for correcting mistakes, but the directive should always come from a supervisor. When it comes to correcting your staff members, praise in public and criticize in private—always. Never allow coworkers to correct a peer, and certainly do not allow them to do so in public. If this happens in your enrollment department, stop it immediately. The team will lose respect for you, the manager, and grow to hate the coworker spouting the criticism. Correctors also listen to every other counselor's telephone conversations and immediately stand up in their cubicle telling another coworker everything the counselor says wrong. They may think they are helping, but they are not. If you allow the situation to continue, you will lose credibility, and your team will see the correctors as know-it-alls.

> When it comes to correcting your staff members, praise in public and criticize in private—always.

 Cutthroat

You can easily identify cutthroats. They think they can do your job better, and they go to great lengths to make sure that every person in the office has heard their opinion. Many serious, well-respected human resources experts will tell you exactly how to manage these people. Numerous authors have written books on the subject of the back-stabbing power climber.

I prefer a simple, pleasant, and self-satisfying solution: Stomp them like a bug, and then get them out of your office. If you are insecure and need their presence to feel good about yourself, then you deserve what they give you. On the other hand, if you are confident in your abilities and know that you earned your position, perhaps you can recommend that these people transfer to another department—today.

No matter how well you hire, you still may find a cutthroat on your team. It happens. Your best defense is to consider attitude carefully during the employment interview. Also, make sure you document, document, and document some more. Your human resources department will frown on you if you want to dismiss someone simply because you do not like the person. You should not seek to do that anyway. However, you cannot exorcise a bad attitude from someone. If you want to hold a bad attitude against an employee during an evaluation, you must document the behavior.

Dedication

We all have our own definition of the term *dedication* based on our career field or position. However, you can easily identify dedication in the enrollment counselor position. Good enrollment counselors need to believe that education can change a life. They need to believe that anyone who wants to go to college deserves the opportunity to try. They need to believe that while many people want to go to college, they may not know how to start the process.

> Good enrollment counselors need to believe that education can change a life.

Enrollment counselors need to understand that they are here to help these people get started and succeed. They also need to believe that the position of enrollment counselor represents a profession and not just a job.

It is not an easy job, and few people have the qualifications necessary to attempt it. Even fewer succeed. When I find people who are highly dedicated to this profession, I want to see them receive a reward; they are truly special people.

Team Skills

Whether you have one enrollment counselor or 50 working for you, they all act as part of a team. They must work together with their fellow enrollment counselors, the academic departments, the financial aid department, and the registrar's office if they want to work effectively. Your counselors' team skills, however, will never matter more than when they work with their fellow enrollment counselors.

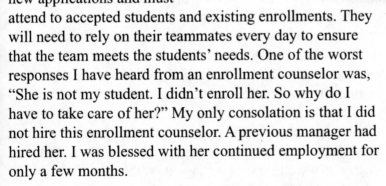

Enrollment counseling is a difficult job. Counselors may need to talk on the telephone for 5 to 7 hours a day. On top of that, they always receive new applications and must attend to accepted students and existing enrollments. They will need to rely on their teammates every day to ensure that the team meets the students' needs. One of the worst responses I have heard from an enrollment counselor was, "She is not my student. I didn't enroll her. So why do I have to take care of her?" My only consolation is that I did not hire this enrollment counselor. A previous manager had hired her. I was blessed with her continued employment for only a few months.

An enrollment team is just that—a team. I stress to all enrollment counselors on their first day that if they do their job well, it will keep them busy. If a coworker needs help, help the team member. I assure the new counselors that the day will come when they will need their team members' help in return.

Good managers need to understand the team concept when looking at the counselors' numbers. I once had a counselor who worked with a student for hours, even though the student was not assigned to her. Since she dedicated so much time to helping the student, she had not been able to accomplish much else that day. She knew her daily activity reports would look bad, but she stepped up to the plate and helped the student through his issues. Not even 2 days later, this counselor had a family (husband, wife, and sister) who wanted to enroll in classes at the same time, and she needed to ask for help from one of her teammates to see the family through the application process. What goes around comes around when working as a team.

> The ability to think and act for the team's benefit matters even more when counselors start to realize their importance to the college.

The ability to think and act for the team's benefit matters even more when counselors start to realize their importance to the college. I always want my enrollment counselors to understand their importance to the college's overall success. When enrollment counselors do their jobs well, everyone benefits. When the entire department does well, employees keep their jobs, the school pays its bills, and the students attending the college benefit from new equipment and new buildings.

I will never tolerate selfish, self-serving employees who think of nothing but their own preservation. It does not matter how well they do personally. If the team fails, the school fails. If the school fails, people lose their jobs and the entire school suffers. Some counselors only understand this reality when I sit them down and show them the gravity of the situation. Sometimes when I would go to troubleshoot a failing campus, I would call a meeting and give the staff members a reality check, letting them know exactly how many jobs and lives were on the line. Sometimes it worked, and sometimes it did not. On the campuses where the reality check failed initially, the new philosophy of responsibility and reward caused some counselors to leave and made other counselors even better. The counselors who stayed wanted to work there and found new meaning in their day-to-day work. Eventually, the disinterested counselors left and new counselors who honestly cared about the college replaced them. In the end, the college and the students won.

Performance Improvement Plans

What happens when you have an employee who does not fit well in the position or in your team? Most human resources departments will recommend a performance improvement plan for the employee. A performance improvement plan is a written plan for the employee's improvement that is based on measurable criteria. Note the key word *measurable*. You want to avoid giving an employee a performance improvement plan that you base on subjective criteria. You also want to avoid setting review periods too far in the future to actually help or giving no deadline for improvement. In the performance improvement plan, I include a target date for improvement of no more than 3 months from the plan's start date. I also schedule an assessment after each month that I expect to see progress.

When you develop an improvement plan, make sure that you make it clear and fair. It cannot simply list actions that you want the employee to take; the plan must also contain a list of items that you, as the employee's manager, will complete to help the employee improve. You want to salvage the employee if possible. The employee should sit in your office as you review every aspect of the plan; in the end, ask him or her to sign the document.

Hire well, train often, and retain your staff.

A piece of advice to new enrollment managers: Hire well, train often, and retain your staff. I have seen so many campuses in the for-profit world fail because of staff turnover. Full recovery from the loss can take a year or longer. Remember, a good, well-trained enrollment counselor can take up to 6 months or more to start to produce. If you do not set the proper expectations from the beginning, provide adequate training, and keep workers motivated, focused, and proud of their work, your department will never reach its full potential.

Chapter Summary

This chapter discussed the challenges that directors of enrollment and enrollment managers face while overseeing an enrollment division or team. It addressed important aspects of the management of an enrollment counselor team, including setting responsibility and rewards, providing accountability and goals for the team, managing team strengths and weaknesses, conducting performance reviews, using performance improvement plans, establishing and measuring a work ethic among the enrollment team's members, and managing enrollment counselors who exhibit difficult attitudes. It also discussed many attitude types and gave suggestions for addressing aberrant behavior. Finally, this chapter emphasized the importance of dedication and strong team skills in competent enrollment counselors.

Chapter
Nine

New Student Retention

This chapter covers the following **key points**:

» Importance of a retention support plan
» Twelve best practices for student retention at online colleges

If you have invested the time, energy, and money into developing an efficient, motivated, and high-producing enrollment team, you need to make sure you have a well-defined and effective retention support plan for your new students after they enroll. High student turnover will kill your program, and nothing is worse than having students leave your college within the first few months of classes. Plenty of good online resources address the issue of new student retention; I strongly recommend that you find them. This chapter examines the following 12 best practices that for-profit and non-profit online colleges use for student retention:

1. Set proper expectations.
2. Provide a comprehensive online orientation.
3. Provide accessible resources.
4. Require faculty accessibility.
5. Encourage active learners.
6. Foster student-to-student interaction.
7. Provide reliable, 24/7 technical support.
8. Make retention telephone calls.
9. Develop and implement an early warning system.
10. Staff a crisis hotline.
11. Offer workshops for change.
12. Require team accountability.

Set Proper Expectations

Setting the proper expectations during the admissions process is important for any college but even more so for online colleges. Most students have a natural expectation of what college life will be like if they attend classes on a brick-and-mortar campus, but students who have never attended an online college have no such natural expectation. They will form their expectations based almost entirely on what they hear from their enrollment and academic counselors.

You cannot wait for classes to start before you tell new students what to expect in terms of posting assignments, answering discussion questions, uploading documents, writing requirements, and the average number of hours they will spend on coursework each week. Different classes will cover different topics, but all colleges should at least prepare and make available to students a day-in-the-life video or presentation. You can also create a mock class or a demonstration course. Regardless of which learning management system you use, you can create a mock class with a generic user name and password. These mock classrooms can effectively put students' minds at ease.

> **All colleges should at least prepare and make available to students a day-in-the-life video or presentation.**

Provide a Comprehensive Online Orientation

Students who have never taken an online class before should absolutely attend a mandatory online orientation, but you can also require students with past online coursework experience to participate in the orientation because different schools use different learning systems. Even if different colleges use the same learning *system*, they may still provide different learning *experiences*.

Since we are talking about an online orientation, you need to remember to make the process convenient for your students. You might want to prepare a PowerPoint presentation or develop an interactive video that counselors can review with students over the telephone or in a chat room. Some schools have developed an orientation classroom using their existing learning system. In any case, remember that most of your new students have no idea what your online college "looks" like. If you prepare your students well before they start classes, you will have a better chance of retaining them.

Provide Accessible Resources

You might want to create a resource scavenger hunt for your online students before the first day of class. Use your demonstration course as a starting point for a class assignment. Then, tell students to find several online resources the college offers and copy and paste screen shots of resource pages in their assignment.

For this assignment to work, you must at least have online resources available to your students. If you offer an online program, then you need to make many of your college resources accessible to your online students. You can also direct students to the many private resources and dozens of different online interactive tutoring sites, writing laboratories, and mathematics laboratories available on the Web.

Provide Accessible Faculty

Brick-and-mortar faculty members must post office hours, and your online faculty members should do the same. Require online faculty to be available via chat room, telephone, or e-mail during a specific time of the day. A few hours a week of dedicated chat-room time will benefit your students greatly.

First-term students often complain about their instructors' inaccessibility. Faculty members do not need to be at their students' beck and call, but they absolutely should be available for a few hours during the week. You would never allow a faculty member on your campus to refuse to have office hours, and you should not tolerate it from your online faculty members either.

Encourage Active Learners

Questions are good. One time, a student called my office in tears because an instructor told her that she was asking too many questions during her first week of class and that she should learn to find the answers herself. I know I may upset many faculty members by saying this, but answering questions is part of your job as an online instructor. Your program chairperson should be ashamed for not letting you know during the interview process what your position entailed.

I understand that every instructor needs to draw the line at some point, but when you have a new online student in the first week of class, you must prepare yourself to answer numerous questions. New students typically feel unsure in unfamiliar territory and need help and support during their first week. After all, we did tell them that we are different and that we have faculty members who care.

> New students typically feel unsure in unfamiliar territory and need help and support.

Foster Student-to-Student Interaction

Since online education is often impersonal, each institution must do what it can to foster a positive, interactive experience. Schools that do this enjoy a high retention rate. Students who feel completely alone while taking an online class often believe they have no personal investment or interest in the experience.

As with your staff members, many students may need to feel like they are part of something larger. If they become part of the classroom team, they will start to see value in their postings and their interactions with other students. If they bond with their classmates and their instructors, they will have a harder time turning their backs and walking away when they have difficulty in a course.

Provide Reliable, 24/7 Technical Support

Online education is not immune to the technical gremlins that live between a student's computer and your online classroom. When attempting any type of technical endeavor, problems and glitches can arise, and online education is no exception.

I know from experience the frustration that these difficulties can cause. When I took a few graduate history classes online, I typically worked on my projects over the weekend and tried to have all of my assignments completed by noon on Sunday. On at least three occasions, I needed to contact technical support because a paper I had written would not upload to my online classroom. I worked 4 hours to resolve one problem. Since I had worked in online education for many years and knew that I would eventually find a solution, I remained calm. However, I can only imagine what new students in the first week of class might feel like if they faced a similar situation. Do not underestimate the value of reliable technical support.

Make Retention Telephone Calls

Voice-to-voice telephone calls are important during the admissions process and irreplaceable when you reach out to students who have already enrolled. At many for-profit colleges, enrollment counselors are responsible for their students' retention through the first week, first month, or even the entire first term. It does not matter when academic counselors take over for admissions counselors in shepherding students through classes. During the first several weeks of a new student's first online class, voice-to-voice contact matters greatly.

Many colleges believe that because they have a good first-course retention rate, they do not need to go the extra mile and reach out to their new students via telephone during their first term. Do not let this belief fool you. Many students who feel frustrated and disappointed during their first class will remain in the program because they have invested time, energy, and money. This feeling of obligation, however, dies quickly. Once they believe that they are alone in their troubles, the damage has already been done and you will not easily regain their respect and trust. If you can catch problems early in a student's first term, you might prevent the student from leaving your college. If you allow the frustration to fester, you will eventually lose the student.

Develop and Implement an Early Warning System

To help students cope with their first term in college, I recommend an emergency e-mail alert system called SOS (Save Our Student). Many times, first-term students do not know how to respond in the face of academic, financial, or personal issues. Some even withdraw from college. If instructors are aware of students in distress, they can use the SOS system to send a specially designed e-mail message directly to a team of retention managers at the college.

Team members include the director of enrollment, the director of financial aid, the student's program chairperson, and the director of student services. To those who say that they do not want to spend time on such e-mails, I must remind them that these students pay our salaries. I would drop everything when I was on the distribution list and received an SOS e-mail. Often, the team can resolve the issue in just a few minutes if the right managers work together on the issue.

Staff a Crisis Hotline

Having a crisis hotline available to your online student is a fantastic idea on so many levels. At most traditional campuses, students have access to personal counselors, grief counselors, employment counselors, depression/ suicide hotlines, and a whole host of other resources. Your online students need these resources just as much as—if not more than—ground-based students. Online students usually feel more alone when a crisis occurs in their lives. Often, they benefit from talking to another student and discussing the problems they face.

Remember, the online modality can be extremely impersonal. If students believe they have no one at the college to turn to, they may give up and leave the college. If you make these resources available to your ground-based students, you should provide them to your online students as well.

Offer Workshops for Change

Change is a way of life in the field of online education. Everything has changed so dramatically since I started working in the industry in the 1990s.

Nobody likes change, especially instructors and students. If you plan to change a learning system or online policy, insist that your instructional staff participate in a workshop or session specific to the change. Instructors often serve as the first line of technical support, and both staff members and students will begrudge your college if the instructors are blindsided by a change they did not anticipate.

Require Team Accountability

Who is responsible for student retention at your ground-based college? I would argue that everyone is responsible. Senior managers, instructors, staff members, counselors, grounds-keepers, janitors, and cafeteria workers all are responsible for servicing your students and ensuring that the school hears and addresses their concerns.

The same people are responsible at your online college. You should not ignore online students just because they do not walk on your campus and cannot knock on your door when they have a problem. If you do not have a retention and student-support plan for your online students, you need to develop one. As a college administrator, you have an ethical and a financial obligation to your board, your staff, your faculty, and—above all—your students. They enrolled in your college because they believed you were different. They believed you actually cared about them. Show them that you do.

> If you do not have a retention and student-support plan for your online students, you need to develop one.

Chapter Summary

This chapter described the importance of creating a comprehensive student-retention support plan for your online college. It presented guidelines for implementing the following 12 best practices for student retention at online colleges:

1. Set the proper expectations.
2. Provide a comprehensive online orientation.
3. Provide accessible resources.
4. Require faculty accessibility.
5. Encourage active learners.
6. Foster student-to-student interaction.
7. Provide reliable, 24/7 technical support.
8. Make retention telephone calls.
9. Develop and implement an early warning system.
10. Staff a crisis hotline.
11. Offer workshops for change.
12. Require team accountability.

These practices apply to any type of institution, and they play an instrumental role in creating and implementing the retention support plan.

Chapter
Ten

The Big Picture

S o, what did we learn? In a nutshell, it's all about the students. You can see it in every aspect and every phase of the enrollment management process—from leads, to initial contacts, to interviews, to acceptance, to proactive follow-up retention practices. As an enrollment manager or enrollment counselor, all students are your students—regardless of whether they were assigned to you or to a fellow counselor. It's about the students. It's not about you. Now, let's retrace our steps to explore more fully what we have learned.

Presence versus Player

When you enter the online education arena, you must make a choice. Do you merely want to have a presence, or do you want to be an active player? You want to be a player, because you care about the students and their educational experience. At the same time, you want a revenue stream. If you choose the presence option, you will count pennies instead of dollars. If you dedicate yourself to being a player in the forefront—which means you have carefully selected, well-planned, appropriately staffed, and fully online degree programs—you can expect to generate a significant revenue stream over the long term.

You've already made one good decision. Your next one matters just as much: Which programs do you want to offer online, and why? It sounds like a simple question, but don't answer too quickly. Remember again that your focus is on the students. Now the answer should be clear. You want programs that cater to the wants and needs of the students living close by—within a 50-mile radius of your college. Online students, many of whom work and already have busy schedules, want convenience. If you provide convenience through your online programs, you will have taken a step toward success.

Now that you know your target market, how do you select programs that will interest prospective students? It's simple. Turn to your school's database. Use it to determine which primary programs have generated the most requests for information from individuals who live within 50 miles of your college. This strategy works because most online students start at a ground campus within the school's 50-mile radius.

To be a player in the online arena, you also need to surround yourself with support staff who put students' interests first. While the quality of your instructors and effective instructor-to-student ratios are essential to making your college one that students want to attend, the enrollment counselors keep the wheels turning. Without their dedication, commitment, and persistence, you might not have enough students to fill your virtual classrooms. Without students, the result is obvious.

The Enrollment Counselor

Your enrollment counselors keep the engines running. Seek them out carefully, and give them the training and resources they need to succeed. If your online programs are not growing—and that is your goal—look to your enrollment counselors. Make sure you have given them an effective initial-contact strategy for working with leads. You want the personal touch—the human-voice contact between enrollment counselor and prospective student— rather than simply an impersonal, automatically generated e-mail reply to inquiries. Students don't want to feel like they are a number; they want to feel like a living, breathing human being whose future matters to the college. Ask your counselors to take a personal interest in each lead and the student's academic success. Online enrollment is more about contacting and bonding with individual students than it is about selling the school, which means that time spent with each student matters greatly. Remember: Those who bond will win.

You may think you don't have time for all of that one-on-one contact—from sorting through leads, to finding the prospects who are truly interested in enrolling, to helping them through the enrollment process, to turning these leads into enrollments. You must make the time. You will fail if you don't. I'm not saying it will be easy. It's hard work. But it's rewarding work—because you will have helped change a life in a positive, long-lasting way. If you surround yourself with a highly trained, dedicated, and professional enrollment staff, you will have the foundation of effective online-enrollment management. Remember, however, that many of the qualities that benefit traditional, ground-based enrollment counselors can prove detrimental in an online-enrollment setting. Do not forget or dismiss the position of enrollment counselor as inconsequential.

> Many of the qualities that benefit traditional, ground-based enrollment counselors can prove detrimental in an online-enrollment setting.

With the stakes so high, you must carefully select your enrollment counselors. You want people who are friendly and energetic and have a positive outlook. You want people who are comfortable with and enjoy talking on the telephone—for 5 or more hours a day, typically. You want persistent people who won't give up on a lead after one telephone call. You want people who have a sincere desire to help other people and can relate to their concerns. You want people who thrive in a pressure-cooker environment on a daily basis. Enrollment counseling is not for the faint of heart or the lazy. So, when you interview prospective counselors, firmly tell them exactly what they can expect while on the job. The stress doesn't drive enrollment counselors to quit; they quit because the pressure is not what they expected. As an enrollment manager, you must hire well. The two basic rules of hiring a successful online-enrollment counselor are to look for the proper personality traits and set the proper expectations. You want to look for something much more important than educational background, degree level, time in previous jobs, or enrollment experience.

An effective strategy is to conduct a telephone interview with job prospects. After all, 90% (or more) of the job involves telephone work. If enrollment counselor applicants come across well during the interview, you can reasonably expect that they will do a good job conversing with prospective students.

A Day in the Life of an Enrollment Counselor

Sometimes they work the day shift, and sometimes they work the late shift. But the routine stays virtually the same at either time of the day. When enrollment counselors arrive at their office, they have two basic—but essential—pieces of equipment: a telephone and a computer with Internet access. They come prepared for a non-stop day focused on customer service. They know that time matters greatly. If they wait too long, another college may successfully lure a prospective student away. Speed of contact and urgency of response separate successful online programs from failed ones.

The day is filled with telephone calls to new leads, old leads, recycled leads, and prospective students with questions about completing the application or about the application process in general or about program offerings. A good enrollment counselor will have little down time. Every minute counts, and every minute of every day needs to be as productive as possible. After a break for lunch, the process continues until quitting time. As always, the enrollment counselor has a list of tasks to accomplish tomorrow, all of which he or she must approach with a sense of urgency.

Creating and Managing Leads

Leads come from a variety of sources, including current students, alumni, college fairs, and your college's Web site. Smart enrollment counselors track all of these leads in their leads database. Your database is a gold mine, so don't let it devolve into a black hole from which old leads never resurface. Doing that could cost you some good students.

Regardless of the source of your leads, you need to act fast. As an enrollment counselor, you don't want any lead to become the fish that got away because you did not respond quickly enough. Make the initial contact sooner rather than later. Once you have the lead on the telephone, however, don't rush. Take control of the conversation. Begin with some informal chatting with the student until you sense that the student has relaxed and knows that you are there to help. Only then should you launch into a series of questions about the student's educational background, current employment status, plans for the future, and education-financing arrangements.

The role of an enrollment counselor, however, involves more than just asking questions. You must listen carefully to each student's answers for clues about which features and benefits your college offers will interest that particular student. Each student presents different wants and needs, so you must tailor the conversation to support the individual. Don't take a cookie-cutter approach; instead, listen, listen, listen.

> Each student presents different wants and needs, so you must tailor the conversation to support the individual.

155

Assume you have gathered pertinent information and the student wants to complete an application. That's great, but don't hang up the telephone just yet. You don't want applicants fending for themselves as they fill out the form. You want to stay with them throughout the process. If any questions arise, you can answer them on the spot. Otherwise, students can grow frustrated, put the application aside, and never return to complete it. When that happens, you lose—and your college loses. So does the student.

That nasty black hole you managed to avoid when it came to leads can emerge again when it comes to the period between application acceptance and a student starting classes. You don't want to go there either, so look out for the following pitfalls: length of time between acceptance and the start of classes, lack of assistance to students seeking financial aid, and little or no post-acceptance follow-up. Many students will feel like they are in uncharted territory. Don't abandon them.

The Online Interview

The heart of the online-student telephone interview is value—for both the college and the student. For the college, the interview serves as an opportunity for enrollment counselors to delve more deeply and examine more closely each student's wants and needs in relation to obtaining a college education and whether the college can meet those needs. For students, the interview offers a chance for them to ask questions—many questions, from the online structure of the college and the cost of tuition and fees to the procedure for applying for financial aid. In other words, the interview presents an opportunity for the student to determine whether your college is a good fit.

This is where features and benefits come into play.

Enrollment counselors must listen carefully to each question and respond with an explanation of specific features and benefits that address the student's specific needs. Every feature has a benefit, and you need to be able to articulate both the feature and the benefit clearly, precisely, and succinctly. Don't assume that a student will know the benefit of a feature just because you do. Also, don't pad your responses with unrelated issues and peripheral fluff that the student will not care about. Remember speed and urgency? You want to get right to the point. You want to build value. The interview serves as a take-and-give exercise: Take information from the student, and give value in return.

The stakes are high, so how do you conduct an effective interview? You can do it all in 10 easy steps: set the stage, bond with the student, gather information about the student's prior education and current employment status, discuss the student's hopes and dreams for the future, offer and describe program options, discuss financial aid availability, specify the cost of tuition and fees, close the deal, and explain the next steps in the enrollment process.

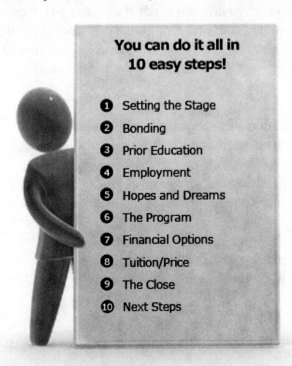

You can do it all in 10 easy steps!

1. Setting the Stage
2. Bonding
3. Prior Education
4. Employment
5. Hopes and Dreams
6. The Program
7. Financial Options
8. Tuition/Price
9. The Close
10. Next Steps

If you don't set the stage properly, the rest of the interview may not go well. You want to let the student know what will take place over the next several minutes, and you want to make the student feel comfortable enough to give you permission to ask questions. Enrollment counselors can learn so much once the student opens up and feels free to address concerns.

Bonding with a student during the interview is a continuation of the bond that the enrollment counselor established during the initial and subsequent contacts with a student. Bonding matters just as much now as it did then. The personal touch matters. Treat students like people—not nameless numbers. If you have hired the appropriate people as enrollment counselors, you should have no problems with this step in the interview process.

> **Bonding matters just as much now as it did then. The personal touch matters. Treat students like people—not nameless numbers.**

When you probe for information about prior education, pay attention to what the student liked and disliked about a prior college. Here again, listen to the student's cues about his or her wants and needs that your college can meet with its features and benefits. You are not trying to assess the student's prospects for success in college. Failure at one college does not necessarily guarantee failure at your college.

The discussion about current employment allows enrollment counselors to hear the student talk about the importance of convenience in taking courses online. Remember to peg the student's reasons to features and benefits your college offers.

A student's hopes and dreams are often related to why the student wants to go to college now. Probe deeply. Don't be satisfied with a one- or two-sentence answer. Gently draw the reason out of the student with whom you have bonded by now.

At this step in the interview process, you should have all of the appropriate features and benefits in mind, and you can now change the focus of the interview from taking information from the student to giving information to the student. You can give information about the program in which the student is interested and answer the questions that nearly all new online students have at this point, such as: "How do online students attend class?" and "What if students need help with coursework?" If you know your college's features and benefits and have at hand the information you need to share with the student, this part of the interview will go smoothly. It offers a further opportunity for you to bond with the student and put to rest the student's fears and anxieties about attending an online college.

Money, tuition, and fees can be uncomfortable topics of conversation, but do not discuss tuition and fees until after you have told the student that financial aid is available (as long as he or she qualifies for it) and that financial aid representatives at your college can help the student apply for and obtain financial aid. If you talk about tuition and fees first, the student will likely begin a silent calculation of how much the education will cost based on a quoted price per semester hour and may decide it will cost too much and he or she cannot attend college. Be proactive. Talk about financial aid first. Unlike financial aid, tuition and fees are more about the value of the service than the dollars and cents. Value does not always mean low price. If you pay more, you often can get more value from your dollars.

The close is when the enrollment counselor seals the deal. If you did your job well, the student will be impressed with your college and want to enroll. But don't hang up the telephone too quickly. Stay on the line while the student completes the application. If you say goodbye and hang up, leaving the student without a source of assistance, he or she may give up in frustration when a puzzling item comes up on the application. Be there to help. Be there for the student. You are adding value.

With that hurdle conquered, finish the interview by describing the next steps in the application process (e.g., acquiring transcripts and letters of recommendation), covering when each item is due, and scheduling a meeting with a financial aid representative. Give financial aid the attention it deserves, or you risk losing an applicant who thinks he or she cannot afford an education.

Managing Conversions

The interpretation of conversion data is a complex and sometimes misunderstood aspect of enrollment management because fallible human beings are involved and managers' experience levels vary along with the related policies at individual colleges. If you undertake the interpretation of conversions, make sure you focus on more than just one or two conversions, such as lead/enrollment or lead/application. Other conversions might pertain more to your college's daily operations. You will also want to track multiple conversions because each conversion tells a different story. You want a panoramic picture—not just a close-up of one aspect of enrollment management. The numbers can tell you where your college is succeeding and where it is falling short—whether in the number of students interested in your college, how many students your enrollment counselors have helped, or how many students are waiting for help. Ultimately, behind every number is a person who needs your help to get a college education.

To paint a comprehensive picture of how your college is faring, stick to the seven basic types of conversions: lead to contact, contact to activity, activity to application, application to accepted, accepted to new start, lead to new start, and application to new start. It may sound like a lot of work, but, if you know what you are doing, tracking the numbers should take no more than about 30 to 40 minutes each day. Before you begin, however, make sure that you have defined your terms and selected a start date and an end date for the accumulation of the data you plan to analyze. Also, make sure you understand that most conversions are rolling conversions and you are looking for a gross number for each conversion type.

> Make sure that you have defined your terms and selected a start date and an end date for the accumulation of the data you plan to analyze.

Tracking the numbers allows you to develop forecasts with the application-to-new lead conversion. This conversion type mixes process with performance and lets you see where you are headed based on current application totals. It also lets you pace the flow of applications to avoid an onslaught shortly before the start of classes. In addition, the forecasting feature helps you calculate how many applications your enrollment counselors will need to acquire per day to reach your goal for new starts.

The lead-to-contact conversion is the base upon which you can build all of the other conversions you want to manage. Without leads and without leads whom you convert into contacts, you will never have activity, applications, acceptance, or enrollment. Turning leads into activities takes persistence from your enrollment counselors. Try reaching leads at different times of the day or evening. Keep trying. Never give up.

The contact-to-activity conversion tracks specific (not general) student requests for action, including interviews, follow-up appointments, and anything short of an application.

You can begin to see the story of your success or failure with the activity-to-application conversion. If your enrollment counselors are doing their job well—following up with their activities, providing interview information to students, and responding quickly out of a sense of urgency—you will likely have high numbers for this conversion. Poor follow-up is a common cause of low numbers for this conversion type.

> Poor follow-up is a common cause of low numbers.

When it comes to the application-to-accepted conversion, never guess about the numbers. This conversion is a direct reflection of your application process, start schedule, and application processing time.

Schools commonly make the mistake of including returning students along with new students when computing the accepted-to-new start conversion. You want to count only the latter—new students. Focus on the term starts—not enrollments. Students continuing with their education at your college are enrolling (again), but they are not enrolling for the first time, which is why I prefer to use the term *starts* rather than enrollments. It is perhaps a fine line, but it is an important distinction.

The most-quoted conversion is lead-to-new start, although it matters only marginally. This conversion will have no real significant meaning until an industry-standard definition of *lead* emerges. If you compute this conversion, make sure you know and understand how you define *lead*. The definition can affect your numbers, and the numbers you get may apply only to your college—and even then, only if you apply the same standard each year. In other words, the numbers will mean only what an enrollment manager wants them to mean.

Calculating Advertising Costs

Dollars spent on advertising to generate leads are valuable. You want to spend them well. All leads—even bad ones—cost money. Don't waste your pennies. Remember also that your enrollment department must own the leads and take responsibility for every dollar spent on marketing. It's a heavy load to carry.

Wise enrollment managers will track their advertising costs per lead type and source. Before you can begin the calculations, you need to prepare your data, dividing your leads according to type and source and creating a column header for each in a spreadsheet. Leads come in many forms, including media leads, referrals, and recycled leads. The latter two types cost no money, which makes them especially welcome. One caution about using recycled leads when calculating advertising costs: Make sure you attribute the lead to the correct advertising type and source. Don't make the mistake of pegging a lead to this year's advertising campaign when the lead actually stemmed from a prior year's advertising campaign. Making the wrong attribution could lead you to the erroneous conclusion that a particular advertising campaign is working when it is actually not bringing in results. Remember, you don't want to waste your advertising dollars on advertising pieces that are not working for you. Recycled media leads are especially appealing because the shelf-life of a media lead never

> Make sure you attribute the lead to the correct advertising type and source. Making the wrong attribution could lead you to the erroneous conclusion that a particular advertising campaign is working when it is actually not bringing in results.

expires. Every time you convert a media lead to a recycled lead, you get back part of a previous year's advertising dollars.

Next, you need to find out the lead sources for each new student who requested information. You want gross numbers. Once you have your lead types and lead sources, you can begin your cost-per-lead calculations. The calculations for cost per application and cost per enrollment work much the same way as the calculations for cost per lead, except they involve application data and enrollment data, respectively. With all of your cost data in place, you can prepare your new enrollment budget and make informed decisions about where and how to spend your advertising dollars.

Managing the Enrollment Team

When it comes to managing an enrollment team effectively, the experience of the enrollment managers plays a key role—particularly in reducing staff turnover. As counterintuitive as it may seem, the constant pressure to produce is not the main reason that enrollment personnel resign from their jobs. Most resign because they do not know the level of pressure from the beginning. Some of the most important attributes to look for during the hiring process include friendliness, an outgoing personality, high energy, a true love of education, and a passion for helping others. Such people can also be difficult to manage. Several strategies can help, including balancing responsibility with reward, setting goals and stressing accountability, focusing on each individual employee's strengths and weaknesses, conducting performance reviews, establishing a bar for work ethic, identifying and defusing attitude problems,

> The constant pressure to produce is not the main reason that enrollment personnel resign from their jobs.

supporting dedication to the work being performed, encouraging team skills, and designing and implementing performance improvement plans when warranted.

Responsibility and reward go hand in hand. Stress to your enrollment counselors the enormity of the job your school has hired them to do. Lives can be changed—for good or for bad—depending on your enrollment counselors' outlook and actions. Assuming that you have hired well, your enrollment counselors will share your vision that they have the power to change a life through education and the power to make your college succeed or fail. They will know that the stakes are high and that the outcome rests in their hands. They will accept the challenge, knowing that with hard work, they can reap the rewards.

> Assuming that you have hired well, your enrollment counselors will share your vision that they have the power to change a life through education and the power to make your college succeed or fail.

The area of accountability and goals is where your conversion numbers come into play. These numbers help you learn where you have been and where you are headed, which allows you to set goals to which you can hold your enrollment counselors accountable. Having daily and weekly goals also helps to keep your counselors on track and focused on the ultimate goal—helping students pursue a college education. Their efforts also bring in cash for the college to keep it running and meeting its students' needs. Keep track of the numbers for your team and for each counselor. Enrollment managers must keep their eye on the ball so they do not miss the target because they never saw the numbers falling short of expectations.

Personal strengths and weaknesses vary from one counselor to the next. All counselors will convert at different rates, and you do not need to correct all of your counselors' weaknesses—especially if a specific strength compensates more than adequately for the deficiency. Work with your counselors—not against them. Take their individual life situations into account. Work styles may differ, but as long as your counselors reach their goals, managers should be pleased.

When conducting performance reviews of enrollment counselors, you cannot make enrollment production the sole—or even the primary—focus of the assessment. The soft skills that each enrollment counselor brings to the job matter more than the enrollment production. These skills are as important as—and perhaps even more important than—quantitative numbers. Soft skills pertain to how your counselors relate to the students they are shepherding through the application and enrollment processes. Four soft skills matter the most: work ethic, attitude, dedication, and team skills. If enrollment counselors excel in these skills, then good enrollment numbers will come in due time.

Work ethic is a subjective term because each individual manager sets his or her own definition for it. You will know that your enrollment counselors have a good work ethic if they do the work they need to do when they need to do it and take care of everything their manager asks them to do.

Related to work ethic is enrollment counselors' dedication to the belief that what they are doing truly matters, that their actions will make a difference in a person's life for years to come, that the people who want to go to college deserve the chance to fulfill that goal, and, above all, that they are here to help others get started and succeed.

Attitude is easier than work ethic to spot and evaluate—especially among employees with bad attitudes. Managing these employees can prove quite difficult. Common bad-attitude employees include whiners (they complain about everything, and nothing can satisfy them; insulate the rest of your team from the whiner, and the whiner will probably produce decently), pointers (they miss nothing and seek out infractions of policies among fellow employees, and they spend the day expending misdirected energy; give pointers a time-consuming task sooner rather than later, and you will be better off), the Ph.D.s (they can be deadly to your team, so put them in their place quickly; they are highly critical and will stick around only until something that they perceive as better comes along), correctors (they correct everyone's mistakes—even in public and in front of peers; they think they are being helpful, but they are mistaken), and cutthroats (they think they can do the job better than anyone else and make sure that other people in the office know of their alleged superiority; solutions to this problem vary).

> Common bad-attitude employees include whiners, pointers, Ph.D.s, correctors, and cutthroats.

While each individual enrollment counselor's work plays a critical role in turning leads into enrollments, counselors cannot forget that they serve as part of a team and that they must share the load when another member needs assistance. They need to know that they can rely on their fellow counselors every day to ensure that all students' needs are met, even if they must help students from another counselor's caseload. Counselors' ability to work as a team also has ramifications for the college itself. When enrollment counselors do their jobs well, everyone benefits. Students receive the services they need, and the college receives the income it requires to further meet the needs of its current and future students.

> When enrollment counselors do their jobs well, everyone benefits. Students receive the services they need, and the college receives the income it requires to further meet the needs of its current and future students.

So, what do you do when you encounter an errant employee? Firing the person is not necessarily the answer. Alternatively, you can develop and implement a written performance improvement plan that is clear and fair. The plan should contain measurable—not subjective—criteria, specified performance review dates, and specific steps the employee's manager will take to help the employee improve performance. You want to try to salvage the employee. He or she can improve.

Retaining New Students

Just because you have enrolled new students does not mean that you can stop your efforts now. You have to keep the students at your school. The 12 best ways to accomplish this are to set proper expectations; provide a comprehensive online orientation; provide accessible resources; require faculty accessibility; encourage active learners; foster student-to-student interaction; provide reliable, 24/7 technical support; make retention telephone calls; develop and implement an early-warning system; staff a crisis hotline; offer workshops for change; and require enrollment-team accountability.

Wrapping It Up

So, now we have come full circle, and you know what you must do to succeed as an online college that works tirelessly to change lives through education one student at a time. Never give up and always believe passionately that with your help, each student can succeed. You want high numbers, but there is more to it than that. It's all about the students.

REFERENCES

Burkhardt, L., & Deeken, M. (2006). *Scheduled and postsecondary education data system*. National Center for Education Statistics. Retrieved from http://nces.ed.gov/ipeds/

U.S. Department of Education. (2007). *Integrated borrower based academic years*. U.S. Department of Education. Retrieved from http://fsaconferences.ed.gov/conferences/library/ nasfaaloan.ppt

Allen, I. E., & Seaman, J. (2008). *Staying the course: Online education in the United States, 2008*. The Sloan Consortium. Retrieved from http://www.sloanconsortium.org/sites/default/files/ staying_the_course-2.pdf

Apollo Group, Inc. (2010). *Apollo Group 2009 Annual Report*. Retrieved from http://www.apollogrp.edu/Annual-Reports/2009%20 Apollo%20annual%20report.pdf